HAPPY 4 LIFE:

Here's How to Do It

By Bob Nozik, MD

Printed in Victoria, Canada

Warning–Disclaimer:
The author and publisher shall have neither liability, nor responsibility to anyone with respect to any loss or damage caused, or alleged to be caused, directly or indirectly by the information contained in this book.

Cover design and illustrations by Kevin Coffey
(cartoonland@pacbell.net)

National Library of Canada Cataloguing in Publication Data

Nozik, Bob, 1934-
    Happy 4 life : here's how to do it / Bob Nozik.
Includes bibliographical references.

ISBN 1-4120-0083-1
    I. Title. II. Title: Happy for life.
BF632.N69 2003   158.1   C2003-902450-4

TRAFFORD

This book was published *on-demand* in cooperation with Trafford Publishing.
On-demand publishing is a unique process and service of making a book available for retail sale to the public taking advantage of on-demand manufacturing and Internet marketing.
On-demand publishing includes promotions, retail sales, manufacturing, order fulfilment, accounting and collecting royalties on behalf of the author.

Suite 6E, 2333 Government St., Victoria, B.C. V8T 4P4, CANADA

Phone	250-383-6864	Toll-free	1-888-232-4444 (Canada & US)
Fax	250-383-6804	E-mail	sales@trafford.com
Web site	www.trafford.com	TRAFFORD PUBLISHING IS A DIVISION OF TRAFFORD HOLDINGS LTD.	
Trafford Catalogue #03-0446	www.trafford.com/robots/03-0446.html		

10   9   8   7   6   5

Praise For Bob Nozik's

HAPPY 4 LIFE; Here's How to Do It

"I can't imagine anyone reading this book and not becoming happier. It's wise, practical and fun. I love it and you will too."
-Richard Carlson, author of *Don't Sweat the Small Stuff*

"This book is a joy to read and is packed with wonderful information that can help everyone become happier."
-Gerald G. Jampolsky, MD, founder of the Center for Attitudinal Healing and co-author (with Diane V. Cirincione) of *Change Your Mind, Change Your Life*

"Written with wisdom, warmth and humor, this book guides the reader, step-by-step back to the only place where true, lasting happiness can be found."
-Jim Dreaver, author of *The Way of Harmony*

"Bob Nozik has gathered into one place the wisdom of the ages about deep, inner contentment and presented it in a highly accessible format. His years of study and his personal story combine to make a dramatic impact. This book is a heartening and compelling read."
-Susan Page, author of *If We're So In Love, Why Aren't We Happy?*

"Bob Nozik has written a lovely, personal book that hits the happiness nail on the head. His exercises are transformative and fun, his stories are a great read, and he has managed to dovetail his own story about happiness with some of the greatest literature and philosophy on the subject. I've read books about happiness and I've written about happiness. This piece is a wonderful addition to the field."
-Rick Foster, co-author (with Greg Hicks) of *How We Choose to Be Happy*

"Dr. Bob Nozik gives the reader a practical and easy to follow road map to happiness. Each chapter is filled with important techniques for self-realization conveyed in interesting anecdotes and personal experiences. If only we could all follow just a small fraction of his advice — the world would be a much happier place."
-Emmett Cunningham, MD, PhD, Professor of Ophthalmology, New York School of Medicine and Vice President of Clinical and Research at Eyetech Pharmaceuticals, Inc.

DEDICATION

To my mom, Helene Nozik Licht who, at age 93, is living in Plantation, Florida with her husband, Ed.

Thanks, Mom, for all your love and for always being there for me. I know the basis for my own happiness comes directly from you.

ACKNOWLEDGMENTS and APPRECIATION

I wish to thank Grant Flint for his invaluable assistance with the writing and editing of this book. And also for acting as my Father Confessor during the tough times. Grant, I couldn't have done it without you.

I also wish to thank Rosie Sorenson, Dr. Joe Michelson, Dr. Emmett Cunningham, Tony Love, and Scotty Rathjen for their tremendous help in critiquing the manuscript of the book.

Many thanks to all the members of NWS (the Naked Writer's Salon) for helping with the in–progress creation of this book.

To my children, Brad and Diane, I want to thank you for your love and support throughout the years.

And perhaps most of all, thanks to Marsha and Jillian for your ever present love and encouragement.

Contents

San Francisco Chronicle

PEOPLE

The Persecution of the Good-Humor Man

He wants to start a support group for the incurably cheery

BY SYLVIA RUBIN

Bob Nozik wakes up chipper, spends his days scripting his good fortune from the rooftops and goes to bed with a smile on his face. Next morning, he's at it again. Chirp, chirp, chirp, all day long, and pretty soon, nobody wants to hear it anymore. So Nozik, a 52-year-old ophthalmologist, ran an ad in a local newspaper saying he wanted to form a support group for happy people.

Bob Nozik is a happy chappy. He wakes up every morning bright-eyed and bushy-tailed. And, he admits, it drives people nuts

Changed for the Better

Everything's Positive

INTRODUCTION

"Hi, Bob, how are you?"

Sounds pretty innocent doesn't it? But this simple greeting changed my life and might change yours as well.

The year is 1987; the place is the University of California Medical Center in San Francisco where I worked as Clinical Professor of Ophthalmology. Passing a colleague on the way to the Eye Clinic one morning, I answered his mundane greeting with a cheery, "Great!" Immediately, his melancholy face twisted into a sneer as he grumbled, "Oh, you're always great!" And, with a dismissive wave of his hand, he fled down the hall.

"Hm," I surmised, "8:00 A.M. and he's already having a bad day."

But this same scene was repeated twice more, almost word for word, sneer for sneer, dismissive hand-wave for dismissive hand-wave.

1

By paring my cheery "Great" to "Okay," I managed to get through the rest of the day without further incident.

At home that evening, I reviewed those encounters with my three grumpy colleagues. They had all found my lively "Great!" annoying. Apparently, being too happy, especially at work and early in the morning, puts people off!

Me, too happy? That's a good one! In the past, no one would have graded my happiness higher than a C-. Still, I was becoming happier. In fact, looking back, I realized that my happiness had been moving steadily upward over the past three years. And this new happiness was qualitatively different as well. It didn't come and go like the happiness I was used to; it was deeper, more solid and reliable than before.

"How strange," I thought, "that it took those three guys at the hospital to make me see how happy I've become."

What's more, subconsciously I knew that displaying too much joy around others is risky. Clearly, I had crossed the line and been too cheerful that morning at the hospital.

How could I have been blind to the major upturn in my own happiness for so long? Could it have developed so slowly that I hadn't noticed? Maybe I thought I was just having a run of good luck. Still, the events taking place during this time of my life had not been unusually good.

Fifteen Minutes of Fame

Mentally, I began to evaluate the happiness of my close friends, family, and coworkers, and quickly concluded that I was now happier than every one of them. "I can't be the only person this happy," I considered, "there must be others. Wouldn't it be great if I could find other people who, instead of being put off by happiness, would celebrate it?"

But how could I find them? Finally, I decided to place an ad in the San Francisco Bay Guardian, a free weekly paper that features a large personals section. Here's the ad I placed:

ARE YOU HAPPY?

Do you find yourself keeping quiet about expressing how wonderful the world is to your friends because they are repulsed by your joy and happiness? We happy people are a group society finds difficult to accept. We need to form a support group for joyful, happy people. Contact Bob Nozik at: (phone #)

When the ad appeared I received a few calls including one from a woman who asked several pointed questions. "Are you promoting some new religion with this ad, one that promises new converts joy and happiness?"

"No," I replied, "I'm Jewish, but secular. I've never been very religious. Besides," I pointed out, "Judaism isn't exactly a new religion."

Satisfied with that answer, she continued: "Are you trying to attract women to date with this ad? Is that what you're really after?"

Although twice married and divorced, I was then already in relationship with the wonderful woman who has been my life partner for more than 20 years. I assured the caller that my ad wasn't a romantic come-on.

She then went on to explain that she was a reporter for the San Francisco Chronicle, the main morning daily newspaper in the City. She liked to scan Guardian ads for material she could turn into human interest stories for the Chronicle. She found my ad to be interesting, and we set a time for an interview.

Three days later she, along with a photographer, arrived at my front door. She spent about an hour asking me all about my happiness and left after taking several photos.

One week later, I was reading the Chronicle and having breakfast at my favorite coffee house. When I got to the "People" section, I was both amazed and amused to find a huge picture of myself sitting in my house looking happy, and a long article about this strangely happy fellow, me.

Now, the phone began to ring, and ring, and ring. My poor, little discount-store answering machine pleaded for early retirement.

One of the calls was from the Associated Press. They insisted on doing another interview and more photos. That story circled the globe. In the ensuing blaze of publicity I got my Andy Warhol's "15 minutes of fame." The *pursuit* of happiness, it seems, is universal, but actually *being happy* is newsworthy!

Happy People, Inc. (HaPI)

I was stunned! If it's true that deep, abiding happiness is rare, how did I, of all people, get it? After all, I'd been unhappy most of my life.

But things were moving too fast to try and answer that one. Riding the wave of publicity, I launched HaPI, Happy People, Inc., a nonprofit organization for happy people. HaPI grew to over one hundred local San Francisco Bay Area members, plus a similar number of national and international associate members. We had a newsletter and threw parties. We also held biweekly seminars where the members discussed how they developed and nurtured their happiness.

As I learned more and more about the members of HaPI, I was surprised to discover that almost 60 per cent were not especially happy. They had joined hoping to learn the secrets for becoming happy.

HaPI lasted just one year. The demands of a busy medical practice plus my research and teaching commitments were too great for me to give HaPI the attention it needed. Nevertheless, I had found my calling. I now knew that once my medical work was over, I would dedicate myself to studying happiness and teaching others how to find it.

Slowly, as I began winding down my medical career, I put more and more time and energy into learning everything I could about happiness.

This book is the product of everything I've absorbed about happiness from self-inquiry, didactic study, as well as what I learned from those members of HaPI who were truly happy.

There are many fine books available which offer a scientific perspective about happiness; however most fail to show their readers how to actually get it. Here you will learn how to **be** happy.

I have but one caution: persons suffering from clinical depression or other serious psychological or psychiatric problems may not benefit from what is recommended here. This book is not an alternative to medication or therapy for mental disorders.

PART I: OVERVIEW OF HAPPINESS

1

Are You Smiley-Happy or Glumbunny-Happy?

*"Happiness is the meaning and the
purpose of life, the whole aim and end of
human existence."*

–Aristotle

Are you happy? Most people struggle when trying to answer this question. They may say: "If you asked me last week I would have said yes, but this week, I don't think so." Or, "I'm not sure what you mean. I'm happier than my friends, Glumbunny and Sadsack, but not as happy as Smiley. Well, two out of three ain't bad, so, yes, I guess I'm pretty happy."

So much for science. About the only way scientists can measure happiness is by asking people if they're happy and how happy. What's needed is a happy-o-meter or happy-scan so they could measure happiness with real precision. "Just look at the bright dot in the viewer for ten seconds . . . that's it . . . good. Congratulations, Smiley, you're a 322! That puts you in the 87th percentile of our happiness study." Or, maybe, "Oh, I'm sorry, Glumbunny, your reading is only 118. You're way down there in the 8th percentile."

No, Really, What Can Science Tell Us About Happiness?

Frankly, not that much. However, data from surveys and interviews suggest that there is a positive correlation between happiness and each of the following:
1) Being married or its equivalent.
2) Being religious or believing in a greater power.
3) Having solid social support.
4) Living with personal freedoms (democracy).
5) Being grateful for what we have.
6) Having work we enjoy.
7) Having happy genes; the offspring of happy people tend to be happy.

Perhaps more surprising is that studies also reveal that happiness is not related to any of these:
1) The amount of money we have; except abject poverty which is correlated with unhappiness.
2) Neither education nor intelligence is associated with happiness.
3) Except for severe, chronic illness, poor health has little effect on happiness.
4) Good looks, alone, doesn't seem to affect happiness.
5) Age, race, and sex aren't significant factors.

The new field of positive psychology (see Martin Seligman's fine book, *Authentic Happiness*) offers hope that one day we will learn much from the science of happiness. Still, without an objective way for measuring happiness, nor, for that matter, even an agreed upon definition of it, science has a long way to go before it can lead us to greater happiness.

Where Do **You** Look for Happiness?

Let's assume that you, like everyone else, want all the happiness you can get. Let's also assume that you've already tried everything you can think of to make yourself happier.

You've;
* tried to get it from work
* tried to get it from play
* tried to get it from sports
* tried to get it from hobbies
* tried to get it from someone else like your spouse, lover, friend, kid, mentor, guru, parent, brother, sister, president, sports hero, spiritual advisor, parole officer, boss, . . . boss? Maybe not your boss
* tried to get it from sex
* tried to get it from alcohol or drugs
* tried to get it from religion
* tried to get it from . . . well, anything else you've tried to get it from.

So how did it work, all that trying? You probably did get happiness from some of your efforts, but not the deep, long-lasting happiness you were really after. Eventually, after years of fruitless searching, you conclude: "I guess happiness is just this little dollop of pleasure I get when I'm lucky, or when I do something well, but it's not meant to last." That's what experience has taught you, right?

Still, some people really are happier than others. Why is this?

Why Is Smiley Happier Than Glumbunny?

Is it simply the luck of the draw? Is it genetics? Do some people just pop-out happier than others? There actually is some science to help us with this puzzle. David Lykken, a well-known research psychologist, found that all of us are born with what he calls a happiness set-point. If you're lucky, you get a high one; unlucky, a low one. Most of us fall somewhere in between.

There's a real difference between set-point happiness and the happiness you get from work/play/sports/hobbies/people/, etc. Set-point happiness is the measure of how happy we are when nothing is either adding to, nor subtracting from our happiness. Lykken compares set-point happiness to the surface of a lake. When something we like happens, it creates a wave which raises the surface of our happiness lake and makes us happier. Similarly, things we don't like create troughs that lower the surface of our happiness lake, causing us to have less happiness.

All we really need to know is that our happiness set-point reflects how happy we are when <u>nothing is either bringing happiness to us or taking it away</u>.

Smiley is happier than Glumbunny because she was born with a higher happiness set-point. When something happens that they both enjoy this happiness adds to both of their set-points. But because Smiley's set-point is higher than Glumbunny's, she will be happier than he is. It's a matter of simple addition.

What's Poor Glumbunny To Do?

So, what can Glumbunny do to become happier? Even though his happiness set-point is lower than Smiley's, he could seek out more happiness from the world. If he likes playing tennis, he could play more tennis. The happiness he gets from playing tennis, added to his set-point, would increase his happiness. If being with good friends makes him happy, he could spend more time with friends. This is what David Lyyken suggests: that we add waves of happiness to our set-point level by doing more things that we enjoy.

But then Lykken says: ". . . these positive experiences cannot permanently raise my set-point, but only produce a temporary wavelike increase that soon recedes to where I started."

So, getting more happiness from hobbies or people or other things we enjoy will only *temporarily* increase our happiness. However, soon we're back pursuing more fleeting happiness. Although temporary happiness is nice, it won't make Glumbunny much happier in the long-run.

What Glumbunny really needs is to find a way to raise his happiness set-point. But is that possible? Yes, it is. Let's eavesdrop on a conversation that may help Glumbunny raise his set-point.

Two Kinds of Happiness

Joy and Norma, two good friends, are having dinner at their favorite restaurant. Let's listen in.

> "Norma, I am so happy we were finally able to find time in our busy schedules to get together! Has it really been six weeks?"

"I know, and I've really needed to talk to you. I'm so confused, Joy."

"What's wrong, Norma? Last time we were together you were so happy."

"I was! I was on top of the world. When Vera gave me the Perkins account, I was ecstatic! Finally, the recognition and responsibility I'd wanted all year. 'Til then, all I got were those stupid little renewals. Joy, when Vera told me the Perkins file was mine, I went straight to heaven!"

Ordinary Happiness

Norma is telling Joy about an episode of <u>ordinary</u> happiness. Ordinary, because her landing the Perkins account is an example of the sort of thing that commonly makes us happy. Norma got something she liked so she became happy. Because it was something she especially wanted, she was ecstatic. Most of us get small dollops of ordinary happiness every day, usually many times each day. Finding a good parking place or eating chocolate will give most of us a little surge of happiness.

Norma's happiness came from her getting the Perkins account, a source **outside** of herself. <u>Ordinary</u> happiness, whether from good luck or hard work, always comes from **outside** sources.

Also, she experienced soaring happiness immediately. There was no delay between her getting the Perkins account and when her happiness began. Ordinary happiness kicks in so quickly <u>we notice it right away</u>. It doesn't sneak up on us.

"So what's the problem, Norma? We both know you have the ability for the job. What brought you down?"

"I don't know. Two weeks after getting the account I just started feeling empty. I know I'm doing good work; Perkins himself said so. I just can't believe my excitement faded so quickly. I keep trying to remind myself of what a big break this is for me, that it could lead to even bigger things. But nothing I say or do seems to help. How could I feel so great one day, and then, for no reason at all, it's gone the next? I'm not depressed or anything, its just back to the old humdrum. Why am I not happy like when I first got the account?"

We all can relate to Norma's feelings. One moment we're basking in the warm glow of happiness, and then, without warning or reason, it's gone. And it seems nothing we do can bring it back.

Norma's experience vividly illustrates several other aspects of ordinary happiness. It never lasts very long. Small victories, like arriving home early because traffic was unexpectedly light, generate brief moments of happiness. Major triumphs like winning millions in the lottery may keep us happy for months. Still, ordinary happiness never lasts as long as we wish it would.

Also, the amount of happiness we get is proportional to how much we value what brought it. Norma really wanted the Perkins account, so her happiness was intense. But, because it's derived from an outside source, she has absolutely no control over how much she gets or how long it lasts.

Ideal Happiness

The second kind of happiness I like to call ideal happiness. It feels wonderful, like its ordinary cousin, but differs in most other ways.

Ordinary happiness is universal. Because this happiness arrives suddenly and unexpectedly, paroxysms of laughter and glee are common accompaniments.

Contrast this with ideal happiness which is experienced as a deep, abiding, inner contentment. Those with ideal happiness may appear outwardly calm and quiet because their happiness has become a part of the totality of who they are.

Let's get back to Norma and Joy and learn more about ideal happiness.

> "Joy, we've known each more than six years, and I've seen how upbeat and optimistic you are almost all the time. How do you do it?"
>
> "Norma, I'm not always cheerful. Remember how crushed I was when Frank decided he wasn't ready to get married? That was less than a year ago."
>
> "Yes, you were upset, very upset. We spent a whole night talking and crying together. But less than a week later you were over it! At first I thought you were just trying to positive-think your way through, but you weren't laughing or making light of anything, you just seemed to look ahead, knowing you would be okay. If it were me, I'd be a basket case for months!"

You've probably figured out by now that Norma is someone with ordinary happiness, while Joy has ideal happiness. Norma sees that Joy's happiness holds firm even through her major upsets. It's not that Joy ignores or laughs away her problems. In fact, she allows herself to experience all of her anger and sadness. But because her happiness is such an integral part of who she is, she is able to experience fully her negative emotions without being overwhelmed by them. By allowing her grieving to run its course, she soon returns to her basic, deeply happy essence.

Unlike ordinary happiness, ideal happiness is enduring. In fact, once started, it's likely to continue lifelong.

Joy's strength comes from deep within her. This is one of the most important characteristics of ideal happiness. And unlike ordinary happiness, <u>it does not spring from luck or good fortune</u>.

> "Well, yes, I guess I did bounce back pretty well. When I finally realized Frank and I were finished, I was sad and angry. But after three days of crying and raging, I was empty; it was time to move on. What I had with Frank was good, but deep down I know life is an adventure. There's lots more joy and sadness for me to experience, and I was ready to pick myself up, climb back on, and ride again."

Because Joy's happiness comes from within, adverse circumstances won't overwhelm her. This doesn't mean she ignores what happens in her world. Quite the opposite. Joy lets herself experience whatever feelings and emotions come up, because her happiness is solid and secure. She knows her negative emotions will pass, and because she allows herself to experience them fully, she <u>recovers much more quickly</u> than someone without her deep, inner happiness.

> "Joy, I really want to know where you get your strength. I know your life isn't any easier than mine, but I usually get so depressed when things go wrong, while you just do what needs to be done and move on even stronger than before. What's your secret?"

Norma senses that Joy's happiness helps her live a full, rich, satisfying life; that her happiness, based on inner strengths, remains fully connected to the realities in her life. Who wouldn't want to live like that?

Ordinary vs. Ideal Happiness

The following table summarizes what we've just learned from Norma and Joy's conversation about ordinary and ideal happiness.

Table: Ordinary vs. Ideal Happiness

	Ordinary	Ideal
How Common:	100%	< 1%
Onset:	Rapid	Gradual
Duration:	Brief	Long
Comes From:	Outside	Inside
Personal Control:	Little	Total
Good Feelings:	Yes	Yes
Can Intensify:	No	Yes

Define Happiness

We've come this far and still haven't defined either ordinary or ideal happiness. When I want a definition, I usually check out Webster or Random House. But the dictionary definition for happiness is so general it doesn't help much: "Fortunate... having, displaying, or marked by pleasure or joy... " And, of course, dictionaries don't subdivide happiness into ordinary and ideal. And lest you think it easy to define happiness, listen to what Norman Cousins had to say about it.

> *"Happiness is the easiest emotion*
> *to feel, the most difficult to define, and*
> *the hardest to create intentionally."*

> – Norman Cousins

"... the most difficult to define... " Still, having looked in detail at the two kinds of happiness, let's see if we can create definitions that will include most of what we now know about ordinary and ideal happiness:

Ordinary Happiness: Largely uncontrolled, intermittent good feelings we get when something happens that we like.

Ideal Happiness: Progressive, sustained, <u>inner</u>-derived contentment we can <u>guide</u> and <u>control</u>.

Notice that these definitions suggest a qualitative difference with regards to the good feelings each conveys. Ordinary happiness creates a sudden joyful explosion, a kind of surface phenomenon. In contrast, we experience ideal happiness as a deep, rich, inner contentment we know we can count on to be there for us.

Who Should You Believe About How to Get Happiness?

I once read a book on happiness where the author laid out a detailed plan he claimed would lead his readers to happiness. However, he then made a startling confession: "… these words are offered from someone whose joy and happiness are probably less than yours." Why would people believe his system would work for them if it didn't help him, if they, the readers, were already happier than he was? I've read many books on happiness and am surprised at how often authors either shrug off or fail to comment on their own happiness.

Many books on happiness are written by therapists who describe ways they have found to help their unhappy patients develop <u>normal</u> happiness. Most of you already have normal, ordinary happiness. You've spent your lives searching out normal happiness. <u>You could write a book on how to get ordinary happiness</u>.

We don't have good scientific information about how happiness develops. So the gold standard for any method must be – <u>does it work</u>? Has the teacher successfully used his own methods for developing and sustaining outstanding happiness for himself and others?

My Story: The Early Years

I was a shy, insecure child with low self-esteem, despite being blessed with supportive, loving parents. I was also rather morose. On a happiness scale of zero being lowest and ten highest, I fell somewhere between three and four. I had the further disadvantage of being short for my age, skinny, and possessed of a nose designed for a larger face. Completing this portrait, I was also a rather indifferent student.

Fortunately for me, my parents thought I was really a beautiful butterfly undergoing my caterpillar stage. However, this upbeat view was not shared by my teachers, as the following incident shows.

Miss Cox, my third-grade teacher, summoned my mother and me to a parent-teacher conference. Although I wandered the classroom feigning indifference, my attention was entirely focused on what the two women were saying. More than five decades later, I still recall their conversation; "Bobby is a nice, quiet boy," Miss Cox said, "he never causes any disturbance in the classroom, but you should know, Mrs. Nozik, that Bobby is a very average student. You mustn't expect too much of him. That would just frustrate both of you." She then added, "His academic potential is low."

Hearing this I felt my heart fossilize and sink into the pit of my stomach. I watched Mom's spine stiffen, her mouth tighten, eyes narrow, as she calmly but firmly retorted: "Miss Cox, you're wrong. I know Bobby better than you. He can do anything he makes up his mind to do." Thanks Mom!

Even with supportive, loving parents, I was not a happy child. And I ripened into a downright unhappy young adult. But I've always been optimistic. I was sure that once I'd achieved my major goals, the happiness of my dreams would follow as surely as spring follows winter.

My dad was a medical doctor and, as a young child, I decided that I, too, would become a doctor. Somewhere along the way, I formed the belief that successful people had all the answers. My dad and other physicians were more than role models to me. Had I simply studied their approaches to success and used them to help me achieve my own goals, all might have been well. But I made their goals my goals, their callings my callings, their life purposes my purposes.

Bitter Success

Sometimes I'd even adopt the quirks and mannerisms of my model *du jour*. I would part my hair the way he did, stroke my chin, frown quizzically, even grow a mustache to actually become whom I was imitating. Quite funny, now that I look back.

But it worked! Becoming the composite of all the doctors I modeled brought me great success. By the time I was 35, my career as an ophthalmologist, mixing patient care with teaching and research, was going well. My lovely wife and I, together with our two beautiful children, lived in a brand-new home in San Francisco, the city of my dreams.

That's the good news. The bad news? I was still not happy. I had been sure that the happiness I craved would follow the success I worked so hard to get. I felt cheated. "I did everything right. Maybe no one is really happy. Maybe this is as good as it gets. I should be satisfied. I have it better than most."

The song, "Is That All There Is?", by Peggy Lee, had just come out. Her mournful lyrics spoke volumes to me. I lay awake for hours night after night thinking: "Is this it? Is this really all there is?"

Slowly I began to realize that what I had achieved was not **"my"** success. It belonged to all those whose lives I had imitated. Woody Allen, in a comedy routine, once said: "They're going to hang me in two minutes and someone else's life is passing before my eyes." What a lesson – that living someone else's life, no matter how well you do it, won't bring happiness. As Aristotle said,

> *"Different men seek after happiness*
> *in different ways and by different means,*
> *and so make for themselves different*
> *modes of life."*
>
> –Aristotle

Finally I got it! I would never be happy unless I followed my own calling guided by my own values. But that meant I had to discover who it was that was living in my chameleon skin. For years I believed I really was the composite of all the stalwarts I had been impersonating. I had lots to learn.

Better Success

Marshaling every dash of optimism I possessed, I began the great trek to self-discovery. Now, as never before, I understood the wisdom of those famous Biblical words of Matthew:

> *"What is a man profited, if he shall*
> *gain the whole world, and lose his own*
> *soul?"*
>
> –Matthew

I started with one advantage, I knew a whole lot about who I **wasn't** and what **didn't** bring me happiness! I had been a resounding success at **not** finding happiness. Thomas Edison once said after repeatedly failing to invent the incandescent lightbulb:

*"Results? Why, man, I have gotten a
lot of results. I know several thousand things
that won't work."*

–Thomas Alva Edison

The next year was the most awful and wonderful of my life. I used everything I knew that **didn't** work for bringing me happiness as my guide. Worldly success was out. So, too, were society's goals and other people's ideas about what I should or shouldn't do or be. I experienced psychotherapy, encounter groups, EST, massage, Rolfing, transactional analysis, Esalen, self-actualization, Gestalt, vision quest, art therapy, various types of meditation, and more. I immersed myself in the entire California mind-body experience of the early '70's. I jumped fully into each new thing I tried, suspending evaluation until my experience of it was over.

And I learned! All those experiences, good, bad, or indifferent, taught me valuable lessons about myself and how to live life. The seeds sowed from that year's experience slowly guided me to the deep happiness I reaped a decade later.

What Now?

What you will learn from this book is a proven way to acquire deep, rich inner happiness. You will learn the secrets that worked for me and for the members of HaPI who were truly happy. And it won't take you a decade of frantic exploration to discover them.

So, if you're ready, lets go to the next chapter where we'll learn just what it takes to get ideal happiness.

2

How Would You Like to Have Your Own Happiness Factory?

"The Constitution only gives people the right to pursue happiness. You have to catch it yourself."

– Ben Franklin

So, how is our friend, Glumbunny, going to prevail over genetics that saddled him with a low happiness set-point?

Your Own Personal Happiness Factory

Glumbunny was born with his own happiness factory. We all get one hardwired into our circuits as part of our "welcome-to-earth" package. This factory arrives, preset, batteries included, to give us a steady stream of happiness; the amount, which varies from person to person, determines the level of our happiness set-point. Smiley came into the world with a high set-point, Glumbunny with a low one. These levels are most likely established either by genetics or just the luck-of-the-draw.

What's important to understand is that it's highly unlikely that any of us, you, me, or Glumbunny, has a defective happiness factory. Glumbunny's problem is that his factory is calibrated to deliver a low happiness output. If he could somehow coax it into producing more, his problem would be solved. One of life's ironies is that we come into the world with all this amazing, hi-tech equipment, but no instruction manual for how to use it.

So, how can Glumbunny get his happiness factory to produce more happiness? Let's brainstorm this a bit.

> **He could research the topic**: Lots of work, and he won't find much practical help.
>
> **He could ask Smiley**: Good idea, after all Smiley's happiness factory is producing well. But Smiley's just lucky; she really has no idea why her factory produces so much happiness. She won't be much help.
>
> **He could use trial and error**: Not bad, it's what I did. But that's likely to take a long time, maybe a lifetime, and he still might not find the happiness he's seeking; after all, few have.
>
> **He could model his search on how he gets ordinary happiness**: Bingo! This approach just might work.

For Outer, Look Outside; for Inner, Look Inside

One thing Glumbunny knows is how to find ordinary happiness. All of us, like Glumbunny, know we can get ordinary happiness from things/people/events outside ourselves. We've already learned that ordinary happiness is characterized by its outside origin. Through trial and error, Glumbunny has already discovered many things that bring him ordinary happiness. Some of the things that bring him happiness are:

Sports cars
Women
Puppies
Tennis
Golf
Days off
Sleeping late
Funny movies
The smell of freshly mown hay
Garlic pickles
Drinking beer with the guys
Babies (unless they're crying)

Glumbunny's complete list is much longer than this, but you get the point. It would be fun and even useful for you to make your own list. What makes you happy?

But why won't anything on his list coax Glumbunny's happiness factory into giving him <u>inner</u> happiness? Outside sources only yield outer or ordinary happiness. Glumbunny will need to work on himself to get his happiness factory to produce more inner, ideal happiness.

Ignition

Now we're getting somewhere. <u>Glumbunny must develop those inner qualities necessary to stoke-up his happiness factory</u>. But which inner qualities, and how can he do it?

There are twelve attributes which, when developed, will lead Glumbunny or anyone else, for that matter, to ideal happiness. I like to call them the twelve keys.

KEYS TO HAPPINESS

1) Conscious Awareness
2) Self-like/Self-love
3) Self-esteem
4) Appreciation/Gratitude
5) Acceptance
6) Responsible Adulthood

7) Non-Judgment
8) Pollyanna's Game
9) Handling Mistakes
10) Individuality
11) Perfection
12) Present-Moment Living

It isn't necessary to master any of them to perfection, <u>reasonable proficiency</u> will start increasing the output of your happiness factory. And, it's likely that you're already doing several of them quite well.

As you begin incorporating more and more of these keys into your life, your happiness factories will rev-up, thereby raising your happiness set-point. <u>Soon you'll be enjoying the happiness you always believed was there for you, but never knew how to find</u>.

So, close your eyes, click your heels and repeat three times: "We're off to find true happiness, the wonderful happiness of ours."

PART II: 12 KEYS FOR UNLOCKING THE DOOR TO IDEAL HAPPINESS

3

"om, omm, ommm"

Wake-up and Smell the Flowers

Happiness Key #1: Conscious Awareness

> *"That all who are happy, are equally happy, is not true. A peasant and a philosopher may be equally satisfied, but not equally happy. Happiness consists in the multiplicity of agreeable consciousness."*
>
> – Samuel Johnson

Hello, Hello! Is Anyone Home?

"You! Yes, you," declared an exasperated Miss Cox, "Bobby, I'm talking to <u>you</u>! "Are you unconscious or just not paying attention? I hope your dreams are good, because if you don't listen–up you won't pass the test tomorrow."

Because I was a dreamer, my frustrated teachers would often scold me. I tried, really I did, but the appeal of what was happening on the other side of the classroom windows always trumped the tedium of school lessons. A stray dog romping in the yard, the allure of a gardener mowing the lawn, or even a loud truck rumbling by, was more than enough to divert my attention. At these times I would just turn off what was going on in the classroom and gaze out the window.

Our five senses – sight, sound, touch, smell, and taste – connect us to our surroundings. These senses bind us to the world and all that's in it. Yet, most of us block our sensory awareness to the point where we spend most of our days in a semi-stupor. Doing this robs us of aliveness.

Let's first examine broad sensory awareness, the least complex kind of consciousness. Attention and inner awareness, the other two kinds, are even more important to our happiness.

Broad Sensory Awareness: A Trip to Greasy Joe's Café

"Glumbunny," Bob announces, "let's go out for lunch. You drive, but notice how you use your senses along the way."

Glumbunny <u>sees</u> his green Honda Accord parked at the curb and, reaching into his right-front pocket, <u>feels</u> the cool, angulated metal objects he knows to be his car keys. <u>Visually</u>, he guides the key, flat side up, into the ignition, turns it hard-right and <u>hears</u> the reassuring grind of the starter as the engine turns over. <u>Looking</u> into the rear view mirror, he guides the vehicle safely into the flow of traffic. <u>Hearing</u> a horn, he slows down, allowing a faster car to pass. While driving, he <u>sees</u> familiar storefronts and street signs letting him know he's headed the right way. <u>Seeing</u> Greasy Joe's sign, he parks in the lot. Leaving his car, he recognizes the <u>smell</u> of roasting meat even before he enters the crowded dining room. His order arrives and he savors the familiar warm, sweet <u>taste</u> of rare hamburger, onion and mustard. He <u>feels</u> the juices run down his fingers, <u>sees</u> the grease puddle on his plate, as he <u>hears</u> other orders sizzling on the grill.

It's now time for the Tums. "Glumbunny, you should really go easy on the grease."

This outing to Greasy Joe's notes but a small fraction of the sensory input we get from all our activities. If you examine Glumbunny's jaunt carefully, every moment occupied several of his senses simultaneously. Convenience and habit will ordinarily block his conscious awareness of most of what goes on. This helps him speed through his day, <u>but at a cost</u>. He is unconscious to much of what happens in his life. He fails to notice and appreciate the wonders of much of the world around him. Most of what he notices are problems and difficulties because they scream so loudly he can't ignore them.

When we view life as little more than a series of unending irritants, our capacity for happiness is diminished. Or, more positively: in broadening our awareness so it includes the quiet beauty and wonder of life, we allow appreciation and gratitude to raise our happiness.

May I Have Your Attention Please?

Harry and Donna are having dinner together in front of the TV.

"Harry, how's your dinner?"

Harry, engrossed in the basketball game, answers flatly, "It's fine, Donna, very good."

"The meat, it's not overcooked? I think it's a little dry myself."

Still not looking up, he says: "No, the steak's fine."

"Harry, it's chicken. You're eating chicken! Remember, we decided to have steak tomorrow, when the kids are here."

"Oh, yeah, I forgot. The chicken's fine... tasty."

"You know, Harry, we need to talk about Hank. I'm worried about him."

"Hank?"

"Yes, Hank, your son! Harry, would you please turn off that stupid game and pay attention to me?"

"Sure, Donna, in a minute... Ohhh! Did you see that? What a shot!"

Sound familiar? Harry is dividing his attention, although clearly, most of it is on the basketball game. Multi-tasking sounds good, efficient, but comes at the cost of weakening our attention, one of our most powerful faculties.

Think of broad sensory awareness as a taking-in process, a gift we receive from our senses. Attention, on the other hand, is more of a sending-out. We direct and send our attention to a person, object, or even to an idea. Sensory awareness is similar to diffuse lighting, illuminating everything within its fall, while attention is like a laser, a beam of concentrated energy. When used skillfully, attention becomes a powerful instrument to help us become more effective, more alive in the world.

Much of the power of attention relates to how it keeps us in the present moment. I first learned to appreciate this power from a pair of old candelabra.

Candelabra Magic

Some years ago, my mom gave me a pair of candelabra. They were old family treasures that she valued highly. Being silver, they required periodic polishing in order to sparkle. To be honest, I hadn't polished them in the several years that had passed since she gave them to me.

Because Mom was nearing 80 and travel was becoming difficult for her, I would usually make the flight from California to Florida to see her. One year, however, she announced that this time she would make the trip to visit me.

Knowing that she would ask to see the candelabra, I pulled them out and inspected them. The beauty of their old world detail and workmanship was evident. But, the film of blotchy-grey tarnish blanketing their convoluted surfaces screamed neglect.

"This won't do," I judged. So armed with a jar of high-quality silver paste, I spent two hours polishing all the surfaces, nooks, and crannies of the ornate rococo.

My attention was focused entirely on that job; no T.V., no radio, and no friends with whom to talk.

After 20 minutes I became aware that I had shifted into an altered state of consciousness. I appreciated, as never before, the incredible beauty of life as somehow reflected and magnified in the metal's luster. My circular strokes released the silver's gleam, leading me to appreciate the cycle of birth, life, death, and rebirth, in an entirely new way; a more spiritual way.

Since that first experience of concentrated attention, I've felt its unique power many times. I've learned that attention can be used for alleviating minor aches and pains, for helping to understand complex issues, and for deepening and enriching feelings of mutual love.

Attention can even project us inward to the portals of our spirituality and our higher selves.

Inner Awareness, the Final Frontier

> *"We are not earthly beings seeking to have a spiritual experience, we are spiritual beings having an earthly experience."*
>
> – Wayne Dyer

"It's all my fault," Glumbunny lamented. "I should have listened to my mother. I stopped attending church on my sixteenth birthday. She begged, even pleaded with me to keep going, but I knew better. Now I'm paying the price. I should have known this would come back to haunt me. That's why I'm not happy, isn't it? It's because I'm a sinner."

Does having happiness require that we be devout? Well, yes and no. Most studies show a positive correlation between happiness and religious practice. However, all that is required is for us to believe in the existence of a power greater than ourselves. Happiness does not favor one religious or spiritual tradition over any other.

It's the Perennial Philosophy, Glumbunny!

"Bob, you're not just trying to make me feel better, are you? Oh, I should have listened to Mom and never stopped going to church."

"If you won't believe me, Glumbunny, let me tell you a little about what's called the perennial philosophy. Its wisdom, which is at the core of all the great religions, has been embraced by sages and mystics throughout human history.

"The perennial philosophy embraces four key points:

"1) There is the world we know through our senses, but also one beyond time and senses, a spiritual world that is eternal.

"2) Despite our physical, earthly limitations, part of us is in contact with that spiritual world.

"3) We are all capable of connecting more directly to this spiritual world.

"4) The highest achievement any of us can have in this life is to connect with the world of spirit."

"So, Glumbunny, religion is just one path, there are others."

"Oh, good. Then there's still hope for me? Please, tell me what I can do?"

Meditate, Meditate, Meditate

Carrying conscious awareness to its highest level asks that we look inside ourselves. We'll need to escape the constant chatter coming from the ego for us to hear the still, quiet voice of our higher self, our intuition. All the great religions and spiritual traditions are united in recommending this.

"Glumbunny, the best way I know for broadening inner awareness is through the regular practice of meditation."

"But meditation sounds so... foreign, so Eastern... not that there's anything wrong with that, it's just that I'm more comfortable with Western methods. Isn't there something Western I can do that would work as well?"

"Meditation is practiced and taught by Western as well as Eastern religions, Glumbunny, but if that seems foreign to you, try using the relaxation response developed by Herbert Benson, a western scientist. That'll work, too. I'll give you a simple technique for this kind of meditation in the Exercise section coming up."

"Well, okay, but I still wish I'd listened to my mother and kept going to church."

CONSCIOUS AWARENESS EXERCISES

Exercises for Broad Sensory Awareness

Exercise: Try going for a walk on a busy street with many shops. Use your senses mindfully. A simple meaning for "mindful" is alert, non-judgmental noticing. It's very important not to judge.   See the stores, plants or trees, people, cars, trucks... take in everything.

Listen to all the sounds, the rumble of moving vehicles, clatter of car doors opening and shutting, the almost musical sounds made by people, birds, and dogs. Even listen for the hum of electricity in over-head wires.

Touch the rough walls of buildings, notice the cool metallic surfaces of parking meters, and the texture of wooden lamp posts.

Step into a coffee shop or café. Notice the smell of fresh brewed coffee and inhale the pungent aroma of bacon and eggs frying on the grill.

Sit down and order something, perhaps coffee and a breakfast roll. Taste the warm bitterness of the brew and contrast that with the textured sweetness of the pastry. Notice how they blend as you hold food in your mouth. See if you can discern the differences in sensitivity of the different parts of your tongue: sweet and salty at the tip, sour along the sides, and bitter towards the back.

These exercises can be done anywhere, anytime. We are engulfed in a cornucopia of sensory richness. As you bring more awareness into your life, notice how much your gratitude and appreciation for what you have increases.

Use mindfulness as you wait your turn at the bank, the grocery checkout line, or while waiting to purchase a ticket at the movies. Try it in your doctor's reception room, when having lunch alone, or while waiting for an elevator.

Attention Exercises

Exercise: Practice attention by concentrating deeply on just one thing; keep your attention *undivided*. Ordinary, uncomplicated tasks that don't require much thinking are best for this. Take your time, at least twenty or thirty minutes.

Consider these for practicing attention:
* Polish silver, brass, or copper objects
* Wax your car
* Weed the lawn or garden
* Study and sketch the veins of a leaf
* Hand wash and dry the dishes
* Volunteer to sweep one of the paths in a park
* Watch a spider spin her web
* Paint a fence
* Vacuum your carpets
* Focus on an ache or pain
* Put all your attention on your lover (this is **very** powerful)

This list just scratches the surface. There are innumerable other ways you can practice attention; let your imagination run wild. The only rules are that your attention should be undivided and without judgment.

Inner Conscious Awareness Exercises

Exercise: Meditation is a simple but effective way to connect with our higher consciousness. Here are some basics:
1) Find a quiet place where you won't be interrupted
2) Sit comfortably in a chair or on a floor cushion
3) Keep your back straight but not stiff; leaning back against the wall is fine
4) Let your hands rest in your lap
5) Relax your body and close your eyes
6) Breathe slowly and naturally from your belly
7) Focus your attention on your breath. Notice as it enters and exits your nostrils
8) Maintain a passive but alert attitude; be mindful.

Expect that your mind and body will need some training at the beginning of your meditation practice.

You may experience back stiffness, neck cricks, nose tickles, ear itches, or other sensations. This is a good time for you to practice attention. When your nose itches, focus all your attention on the itch. Silently say: "Nose itching, itching, itching, itching… " Focusing your attention will usually cause the itching to stop. Of course, you could just scratch it. But that may precipitate more itches, then tickles, or burnings, or even twinges that move from nose to ear to forehead to the back of your hand, and so on.

In any case, these annoyances will usually fade away after only a week or two of regular meditation practice.

It's likely that you'll also need to train your mind when you begin meditating. You'll think thoughts like: "I'm doing this all wrong. This is silly. I hope Jack remembers to get milk on his way home. I'll take a peek at the time... what? Only four minutes? This is hopeless."

You'll understand why Buddhists say we have monkey-minds, with all this ceaseless chatter. Let your thoughts move right through your consciousness. Don't become attached to them; just release them. Thoughts are just thoughts, nothing more; you needn't believe them nor become trapped in their <u>drama</u>. It's best to mindfully observe them as they pass through your consciousness.

It may be helpful for you to label any persistent thoughts. "Thinking of car repairs ... thinking of car repairs ... thinking ... thinking." And then let them go. Don't judge them and don't try to suppress them, just notice them and release them.

As you continue your meditative practice, you will find your mind and body will adapt better and better.

❀ ❀ ❀ ❀ ❀ ❀

"Glumbunny, meet Glumbunny."

"Glumbunny, now that you are becoming more aware of your surroundings and yourself, I'd like to introduce you to your best friend."

"Oh, you probably mean my good friend, Smiley."

"No, Glumbunny, Smiley is a good friend, but in the next chapter you'll meet your one and only **best** friend."

4

" I LOVE ME
SOOOO MUCH! "

Love and Kisses to Me

Happiness Key #2: Self-Like/Self-Love

*"To love one's self is the beginning of
a lifelong romance."*

– Oscar Wilde

It may be possible for a person to be happy if she doesn't like or
love herself, but I've not seen it. Think about it. You're with yourself 24/7
from birth to death. You are the only one who knows you inside and
out, your innermost motives, most cherished values, fondest dreams.
Yet most of us invest little time or effort in the most important relationship we will ever have – the one we have with ourselves.

What is Self-Like?

Liking yourself means that you enjoy spending time with your self; enjoy it so much that you become your own best pal. "Well, Duh!" you might say. "Since I'm with myself all the time, doesn't that automatically make me my best friend?"

Actually, no, it doesn't. Despite the anatomical linkage, most of us find all sorts of creative ways for avoiding real contact with ourselves. We may surround ourselves with other people to escape our fear of being alone. Or we may become workaholics in order to avoid ourselves. Alcohol and drugs may be used to escape ourselves. Filling our hours with mind-numbing television works well, too. And these are just some of the ploys used to dilute the time we spend with ourselves.

Inner-Critic

It is difficult to like ourselves when the voice inside our own head is disrespectful or insulting. Let's listen to the way Glumbunny's inner-critic speaks to him.

> "Glumbunny, do you like yourself?"
>
> "Gee, Bob, I don't know, sometimes I do, but other times not very much."
>
> "Let me put it this way – last week when we went to Greasy Joe's for lunch, you made a wrong turn on 21st street, do you remember?"
>
> "Yeah, I still can't believe I did that. I go there all the time. When I screw up like that, I really get mad at myself, especially because I know better. I hope you're not mad at me; did I make you late for something?"
>
> "No, not at all, but when that happened, what did you say to yourself?"
>
> "Well, something like, 'You moron! Can't you do anything right? How can you turn a simple trip to Greasy Joe's into such a disaster? Bob's going to think you're an idiot!'"
>
> "And what was the tone of that inner voice?"
>
> "Harsh… stinging! When I do stuff like that, I really get on my case. I called myself every name in the book, along with a few that aren't in the book."

Glumbunny is hard on himself, but this kind of self-flagellation goes on inside many of our heads when we make mistakes. Eventually, we may become so accustomed to this insulting self-talk that we fail to notice its rude disrespect. But that doesn't stop the damage it causes to our feelings of self-like and love.

The inner-critic develops during our early years. It reflects the voices of our angry parents, judgmental teachers, or others who were critical of us while we were growing up.

Children need guidance while learning to be effective in the world. But children whose life lessons were accompanied by insults and put-downs often grow into adults with low self-like, who believe every nasty thing their harsh inner critic tells them.

By acquiescing to the abuse of our inner critic, we become devalued in our own eyes. We see ourselves as pathetic, unlikeable, and unlovable, and not surprisingly, our happiness suffers.

Taming the Beast

Taming our inner-critic begins by just listening to it. Listening mindfully, noticing the words and tones it uses as it gets on our case. I remember when I finally woke to the harshness of my own inner-critic.

It was a glorious time to be on the golf course. The sun had been up less than an hour and dew still glistened on the freshly mown fairways. Layne, my every-Friday-morning golf buddy, and I were locked in a tight match. It was the 8th hole, a long par four with a deep canyon on the right. I was one stroke behind. We both drove down the middle of the fairway, but I was about ten yards ahead of him. His second shot found the trap, left of the green.

"Oh, too bad!" I lied. What I meant was, "Good! We'll soon be all square." Lining up the shot and taking my stance, I silently repeated my back-swing mantra: "Remember now! Eyes on the ball, firm left elbow, swing easy."

All was forgotten on the downswing. My head turned prematurely as I lunged violently forward, almost falling off my feet. The four iron gouged a sardonic grin into the face of my titleist-3, propelling it straight into the canyon.

Barely hearing Layne's disingenuous, "Oh, too bad!", my inner critic screamed: "You STUPID IMBECILE!!! Can't you do anything right! You don't deserve to live! You're pathetic!"

This was too much. Finally, I saw the red-faced, vein-popping demon in my head for what he was. Bringing this hysterical inner-critic before the jury of my own awareness, marked the beginning of the end of its long reign of terror.

Inner-Colleague

So, is the inner-critic nothing but a worthless irritant? Should we surgically extract it like we do our vestigial appendix when it's inflamed? No, a respectful inner-critic can be very useful. Once tamed, it can help us with many of our daily tasks. But we need to take control over our inner-critics; teach them their proper role in our lives. And certainly, they must learn manners. This will turn our inner-critic into what I call an inner-colleague.

Here's an example of how my inner-colleague recently helped me replace a worn lamp cord.

> (Inner-colleague) "Ah, Bobby, we're home early, good time to replace that beat-up old lamp cord, what do you think? Great! We just need to get everything together, new cord and plug assembly, wire strippers, electrical tape, I think that's everything.
>
> ✻ ✻ ✻
>
> "Gee, I know you want to live a long life so maybe you'd better unplug the lamp before we start. That's it. Hmm, maybe spread newspaper under your work area, you know how you hate picking little black things out of the carpet.
>
> ✻ ✻ ✻
>
> "Don't be too aggressive about cutting the old wire close to the base or you might have to do microsurgery to connect it to the new cord.
>
> ✻ ✻ ✻
>
> "Best to check first to be sure this new cord is long enough. Ahh, perfect!
>
> ✻ ✻ ✻
>
> "Okay, just strip an inch of insulation off the new cord and the remaining old one. Any more and you might not have enough electrical tape to cover it. Good! I don't know if it matters in this case, but maybe play it safe and connect bronze to bronze and silver to silver.

Yeah, use a little extra tape so there's no chance the
bare wires will touch."

＊ ＊ ＊

"Hey, looking good; but let's test it first just to be
sure everything's working before running the cord behind all the furniture. Good job! A quick clean up and
it's martini-time."

Okay, so my inner-colleague's a bit of a wise-guy, but I think he's
funny and I trained him to be like that. You can train yours to be any
way you like. Just be sure his words and tone are respectful. <u>This is
what distinguishes an inner-colleague from an inner-critic</u>.

Turning a strident inner critic into a good-natured, helpful inner-
colleague is not difficult. The exercises at the end of this chapter will
help lighten-up even Glumbunny's inner-critic.

Self-love

One step up from self-like is <u>self-love</u>. Self-love is very much like
the love that develops between two people. While attraction, even
infatuation can occur instantaneously, true love requires the lovers to
know each other well, deeply. Similarly, self-love is based upon self-
knowledge.

> *"Resolve to be thyself; and know
> that he who finds himself, loses his mis-
> ery."*

> – Matthew Arnold

I wonder if Glumbunny knows very much about himself?

"Glumbunny, how well do you know yourself?"
"As well as I want to; I mean, some things are better not to know, aren't they?"
"For example... ?"
"Well, negative things. Sometimes I get angry and
don't know why. I had a fight with my wife two days
ago when she kept asking if something was bothering
me. It really got to me that she wouldn't just let me be.
Sure, I could probably dig down and find stuff about
myself, maybe upsetting things, negative things. What
good would that do? It would probably just worry me
and everyone else.

"All in all, I think I'm a pretty good person," Glumbunny continued, "but, sometimes it's best not to know everything. What if I found something ugly about myself, some old, buried stuff that I couldn't do anything about anyway? What's the good in picking the scabs off old wounds?"

Warts and All

Glumbunny asks a good question. Do we really need to excavate and examine everything buried inside us in order to love ourselves?

Self-discovery does take courage. It's scary to dig deep, probing for who we are. We might find something we don't like, something dark or ugly.

Most of us are trained from childhood to try to fulfill other people's ideals of perfection. And, failing to meet those unattainable standards of plastic perfection, we feel flawed and unlovable the way we are.

So we try and paper over our so-called imperfections, hiding them from ourselves and others. Yet, subconsciously, we know our flaws are still there. For the 99.9 per cent of us who are not psychopaths, what lies hidden are just qualities and preferences that, if expressed, would actually make us more interesting, not unworthy of love; whether self-love or the love of others.

Discovering who we are means we must remove the lids from long-sealed jars. But it's well worth it. Self-love depends upon our knowing who we really are, warts and all.

I know what I'm asking of you is difficult. Still, without knowing who you are, how can you expect to love yourself?

Frank's search to know himself uncovered a very unwelcome surprise. Let's see how he dealt with it.

Frank's Painful Discovery

Frank was determined to learn who he really was, because not knowing hadn't worked; he was miserably unhappy. Still, fearing what he might find, he was apprehensive.

Mike, a guy he barely knew, invited him to some "big event" going on in Cotati, a small town an hour north of San Francisco. Although Mike refused to provide any details, Frank thought, "What the Hell," and decided to go.

When he got there, the big barn of a building was already occupied by perhaps forty young men and women all seated on folding chairs arranged in a circle. Shortly after he arrived, various people began telling the assembled group about themselves. One of them, a short, pudgy guy in horn-rimmed glasses, disclosed that he was trying to get in touch with his feminine side.

Frank decided this must be a leaderless encounter group, an event that was not uncommon in the San Francisco Bay Area in the early '70's.

After an hour or so, Rex, a man of about 40 or 45, stood up and announced in a loud voice, "I suppose you're all wondering what this is all about." Rex was tall and good-looking in a dark, brooding sort of way.

"I'm the leader of a group that meets here regularly," he announced, "and most of you were invited by our regular members because we want to expand our circle." He asked all of the members to stand. A score of fresh-faced young men and women dispersed throughout the circle jumped to their feet.

"We believe" he continued, "society is going to Hell because men are becoming like women and women are trying to be men."

"Yeah!" shouted one of the male members pointing to the short fellow in the horn-rimmed glasses. "It really pissed me off listening to this guy's garbage about getting into his female side!"

Two other male members shouted: "Me, too!"

The little guy, now sweating profusely, stammered: "But... a... bbut I didn't mean... "

Rex challenged, "He pissed you off, so what are you going to do about it?"

"I'm gonna' throw 'im out-a-here!"

With that, the three angry members charged the little guy, beating him, breaking his glasses, and then literally threw him out of the building.

Frank, watching the assault, was transfixed. He made no attempt to stop it, but knew he wanted nothing to do with Rex or his crypto-Nazi group.

The weeks following the Cotati caper were hard for Frank. But he forced himself to examine all that had happened, and his tolerance of the violence he had witnessed. Honesty forced him to admit that there was a part of him that enjoyed watching the beating. He was appalled. How could he claim to be a good person knowing this about himself? How could he ever love, or even like himself?

Looking back over his life, Frank realized that he had never knowingly hurt anyone. He began to see that what he was accountable for was what he <u>did</u> in life, not for his thoughts or fantasies. What's more, he realized that he could direct his fantasies in ways that were safe and responsible so no one would be harmed.

Today, Frank enjoys watching wrestling and boxing matches, and is an avid football fan. He has channeled his attraction to violence in ways which satisfies him, but causes no harm.

The violence-enjoying part of him was hard for Frank to accept, but acknowledging this part of himself was necessary for him to develop the self-love necessary for his happiness.

SELF-LIKE/SELF-LOVE EXERCISES

Self-Like

<u>Exercise #1</u>: Convert your inner-critic into an inner-colleague. This simple but effective exercise requires two steps:

* Step #1: Listen to the way your inner critic speaks to you. Pay attention to its words and tone. Is its voice sarcastic or insulting? Does it scream insults at you every time you make a mistake? Listen consciously, mindfully. Don't judge, just listen. Your inner critic has been with you so long that you've probably adapted to its disrespect.

    Do this for two weeks. Just listen; don't try to stop or change it. Don't even judge no matter what it says or how it says it. Certainly don't judge yourself for you putting up with it so long; after all, you are doing something about it now.

* Step #2: Now that you are conscious of its words and tone, it's time to change it.

    Every time your inner-critic begins haranguing you, stop it in its tracks. Say something like: "Don't talk to me like that! Speak <u>nicely</u> to me." Don't permit any sarcasm or insults. When you're alone, do this out loud and speak forcibly. Insist that it treat you respectfully, no matter what you've done. Do this, and within a matter of weeks, your inner-critic will be magically transformed into a helpful, respectful inner-colleague.

I've encouraged my own inner-colleague to develop a playful, humorous voice. You can train yours to have whatever tone you like.

Exercise #2: Become your own best friend.

Friends spend quality time together. They have fun with each other. Here is a list of some things that will help you become best friends with yourself.

Make a date with yourself for an evening or even a whole day. You could:

* Take yourself out for dinner at a nice restaurant
* Spend an afternoon at a museum
* People-watch (for fun, imagine what their life-stories might be)
* Work on a hobby
* Roam around a new neighborhood seeing if you can capture its essence
* Go to a city park and watch the dynamics of children at play
* Go on a spiritual retreat
* Hike into the mountains or a nature preserve
* Throw a few essentials in the car and just take off without any particular destination. I love doing this one.

Use your imagination. Almost anything you might do with a good friend you can do with yourself. Use internal dialogue as if you were having a conversation with a good friend.

Passive activities like watching TV, going to movies, or even reading a book, are less good for this exercise. Best are those activities that promote inner dialogue.

Self-love

Exercises that help you know yourself better promote self-love.

It's best to approach these exercises with a spirit of adventure, the adventure of self-discovery.

As with any adventure, expect that you'll find fear mixed in with the excitement and exhilaration. In fact, fear is a clue that you're on the right track; don't let it stop you. Author Susan Jeffers says, "Feel the fear and do it anyway." This is excellent counsel for this work. Trust that the good feelings coming from the self-love you create will be well worth any fear you experience along the way.

Exercise: The following exercises will help launch your self-discovery adventure:

* List those things you like doing
* List things you would like to do if no one were watching.
* List what you would like to do if there were no negative consequences.
* List those things you find upsetting.
* If you could be anyone who ever lived, who would that be and why?
* List what you most dislike about yourself and why.
* Working with a close friend, ask them:
  "What are my strong points?"
  "What are my weak points?"
  "What do I hide from others?"
  "What do I hide from myself?"
  (Accept without judgment whatever answers they give as information that may help you, even if you disagree.)

Anything you find upsetting coming from these exercises is a clue about your hidden self. We don't easily accept as true what we've kept concealed from ourselves. Remember, you needn't <u>like</u> what you discover, but you do need to <u>accept</u> it. Some of what you uncover about yourself, you will like and enjoy. But, as Frank discovered, you may find other aspects of yourself you'll want to recast. In either case, <u>discovery and acceptance are necessary first steps to cultivating true self-love</u>.

Once again, your best approach is to mindfully notice whatever appears, without judgment.

Just as true love between two people is predicated upon each of them knowing the other well, self-love springs from self-knowledge.

✳✳✳✳✳✳

"Aren't self-love and self-esteem the same?"

"I just noticed," Glumbunny interjects, "that the next chapter is about self-esteem. I've always thought of self-love and self-esteem as being interchangeable."

Glumbunny, many consider self-love and self-esteem to be the same, but they're not. Let's move right on to Chapter 5 where you'll learn how they differ and why you should care.

"NEXT TIME
I'LL BUILD AN EVEN
BIGGER ONE!"

You Can Do It, I Know You Can

Happiness Key #3: Self-Esteem

> *"To trust one's mind and to know that
> one is worthy of happiness is the essence
> of self esteem."*

> – Nathaniel Brandon

What is self-esteem and how does it differ from self-love?

The best way for me to demonstrate their differences is to introduce you to two new people.

First meet Trudy, a friend I've known for more than 20 years. An attractive forty-something divorcee, Trudy

45

is constantly flying off in all directions. Years ago she took a personal growth seminar and spent the next six years as an unpaid seminar assistant.

For health, she eats only macrobiotic, organic foods, while at the same time chain-smoking Virginia Slims. She takes 15 to 20 herbal remedies every day to strengthen her immune system, aid digestion, raise energy and enhance orgasm. The fact that there is no research to support these claims doesn't dampen her enthusiasm.

Trudy quit her job several years ago because her employer didn't want employees smoking dope on the job. She then became a full-time folk singer working in clubs for tips.

Recently, a friend convinced her to invest a large portion of her life savings in a pyramid scheme. Now the money's gone and the friend doesn't return her phone calls.

Through it all, she remains optimistic and in good spirits convinced "the Universe will provide." Trudy is so sweetly sincere that her friends happily rescue her whenever she needs help.

Trudy is adorable. She seems almost too innocent for this rough-and-tumble world. She's a loyal friend who is unfailingly honest and well-meaning. She has many friends who love and enjoy her company.

While likeable, even loveable, Trudy does not command respect. Respect is essential for esteem, whether directed at others or ourselves.

Self-esteem is an inner quality, a sense or feeling that we are capable of dealing effectively with whatever life presents.

Now meet Runyon. You'll find Runyon to be very different from Trudy.

Runyon, a professional colleague I've know nearly 40 years, retired ten years ago. He was a brilliant innovator who rose to the top of his field. Runyon was also a tyrant. He surrounded himself with yes-men who would tiptoe around the great man, fearing at any moment they would be nailed by his disapproving eye. In an instant, Runyon could transform a subordinate into a helpless, squirming insect skewered to the wall by his pointed verbal barbs. I once saw him reduce a colleague to tears, with a publicly administered tongue-lashing.

But his work was dazzling. There is less blindness in the world today because of Runyon.

Do I respect Runyon? Yes! Do I esteem Runyon? Absolutely! But I don't like him and would never spend any off-hours with him if I could avoid it. He's too unpleasant to be good company, and I find his lack of respect, consideration, and kindness for others to be contemptible.

Trudy – we don't respect (but like). Does she have self-respect? I doubt it.

Runyon – we respect but don't like. Does he have self-like? Probably not.

There are many, like Trudy and Runyon, whose self-like/love and esteem qualities are out of sync.

What Is Self-Esteem?

"Self-esteem is the disposition to experience oneself as competent to cope with the basic challenges of life and as worthy of happiness."

– Nathaniel Branden

"Doesn't self-esteem," Glumbunny protests, "come from doing good, effective work? Branden's definition makes it sound like it's just a state of mind."

Many believe we develop high self-esteem by doing things well in the world. Actually, it's the other way around. Having self-esteem helps us do better work and achieve more.

High self-esteem lets us know that we will meet whatever challenge life gives us responsibly and with our best effort. High self-esteem helps us view any poor results we get as learning opportunities rather than crushing defeats.

Implicit in the term self-esteem is the notion that we live our lives in congruence with our values. So if personal honesty is one of our values, but we cheat on our income tax, or pad our expense accounts, or even "forget" a few strokes on our golf scores, we are not living congruously with our values, and our self-esteem will suffer.

What About Performance?

*"There's something wrong with a
system that doesn't reward superior pro-
ductivity with greater self-esteem."*

– Glumbunny

Many of us feel as Glumbunny does that possessing superior intelligence along with excellent training and work habits should guarantee us greater self-esteem. Certainly good work often leads to material success. And while being productive on the job won't diminish it, without the proper inner work, it won't raise self-esteem either.

Let's take a closer at Glumbunny to see why this is so.

Glumbunny, a 46-year-old junior executive in a large advertising agency, lives with his wife and two teenage girls in a nice older house in the suburbs. By his own admission, Glumbunny is a workaholic. He's also a nervous wreck. Although highly skilled, he's been passed over for several promotions because he has difficulty working with others. He expects them to match his compulsive perfectionism and long work days.

He's also overweight, has high blood pressure, late-onset diabetes, angina, and carries a total cholesterol of 328. He hasn't taken a vacation in almost three years. His wife is in therapy because she feels ignored and not understood by Glumbunny. He spends little time with his family because he's always at the office.

Work is where Glumbunny shines. He has a number of important clients but lives in constant fear that he might lose them to his competitors. He landed a big new account last week, but after a few hours of private celebration, began to worry that he wasn't good enough to hold on to it.

Glumbunny has talent and ability. He's a productive executive with a leading advertising agency. Still, low self-esteem is damaging his personal relationships, limiting his business success, and harming his health and happiness. Sadly, the combination of high ability and low self-esteem is anything but rare.

Pseudo Self-Esteem

Some people try to hide their feelings of low self-esteem from themselves and others. Fearing something must be terribly wrong with them, they fall into denial and present themselves to the world with overblown self-confidence and bravado. This deception just adds to their inner feelings of despair and panic.

When our self-esteem is strong, we have less need for outside approval. Those with weak self-esteem constantly seek approval from others. But no matter how much they get, it's never enough. And criticism often leads them to rage or depression.

SELF-ESTEEM EXERCISES

Exercise #1: Rate your own self-esteem.

You probably know whether or not you have a problem with self-esteem. However, if you put lots of energy into maintaining a flashy self-image, you may be invested in pseudo rather than true self-esteem. Recognizing this is a very important first step in freeing yourself from this trap.

Carry a notebook with you and record any negative thoughts you have about yourself as they come up. Your list might look something like this:

> I'm such an idiot! Why do I always forget where I put my keys?
> I'm so boring that nobody ever wants to talk to me at parties.
> Why do I always say such stupid things to my boss?
> I'm hopeless at math. I can't even balance my checkbook.

These statements arise from the beliefs you've formed about yourself years ago. These beliefs resulted from recurring negative thoughts you had during your formative years. While there is often a germ of truth to them, they become more and more generalized and distorted as the years roll by. And intense negative thoughts and beliefs repeated over and over again are devastating to your self-esteem.

Learning to listen to your negative self–talk is the first step to reducing its negative effects.

Exercise #2: Correcting negative self-talk.

Now that you've become aware of it, critically examine each of your negative beliefs about yourself and rephrase them to more accurately reflect reality. Be honest. Don't change "I'm hopeless at math" to "I'm a mathematical genius." Say instead: "With care, I can correctly perform basic mathematical calculations."

Toxic self-talk must be stopped if you are to raise your self-esteem. As you change your negative self-talk so that it more correctly matches the truth, your self-esteem will grow.

If, after doing these exercises, your self-esteem is still low, consider seeking professional help. Persistent problems having to do with self-esteem may impede your progress towards happiness.

❈ ❈ ❈ ❈ ❈ ❈

High levels of self-like/self-love and self-esteem will help us see and appreciate who we really are. And with that appreciation, the happiness we seek will be much closer.

We are now ready to go on to the next happiness key, Appreciation/Gratitude. This is the key that will help us awaken to the cornucopia of wonders that fill all of our lives.

6

"THANK YOU, THANK YOU, THANK YOU!"

Count Your Blessings and Remember to Say Thank-You

Happiness Key #4: Appreciation/Gratitude

Most human beings have an almost infinite capacity for taking things for granted.

– Aldous Huxley

Gratitude is the sign of noble souls.

– Aesop

The twin virtues, appreciation and gratitude, are honored by inclusion in all of the world's religious and spiritual traditions.

It's hard to imagine having one without the other. Appreciation comes from recognizing and treasuring what we have, while gratitude is expressing thanks for it.

Just a minute, I think Glumbunny has something to say.

> "First, I want to say that I've been doing the awareness, self-love/like, and self-esteem exercises. I'm really surprised! I'm already noticing more of everything around me, my inner critic is less insulting, and I'm enjoying my own company more than I ever have.
>
> "My self-esteem is still not where I'd like it to be, but it's starting to improve and the exercises are helping. At first I though they were too simple, but hey, they work!
>
> "I know I'm fortunate to live where I do, that I have a nice family, and a good job. I think my level of appreciation and gratitude is already pretty good. How 'bout if I skip this chapter to save a little time and take up one of the keys that I know are hard for me?"

Glumbunny raises an important issue. Are unhappy people, like Glumbunny, deficient in all the happiness keys? And if not, is it okay for them to skip their strong ones and just work on their weak ones?

In fact, it's not just possible, but likely that Glumbunny is handling one or two of them well already. But these keys are interrelated, and often the easiest way to improve a weak one is by making a strong one even stronger.

"So, no Glumbunny, don't skip any of them."

Appreciate What?

Appreciation is closely related to conscious awareness. Awakening our awareness to the wonders of our inner and outer environment helps us build appreciation. The conscious awareness exercises at the end of Chapter Two will also help us with appreciation and gratitude.

The gift given each and every one of us, this life on earth, is a blessing beyond human comprehension. In the face of astronomical odds, each of us was selected to receive this miraculous prize. How could we not awaken each morning awash in appreciation and gratitude? But most of us view life as little more that a series of unending burdens that fill our time with suffering and disappointment.

"The Mass of Men Live Lives of Quiet Desperation"

–Henry David Thoreau

Most of us believe our lives must have favorable circumstances before we can be appreciative. But there will always be things about our lives we don't like. And because we put so much energy into what we want but lack, most of us have little left to appreciate the wealth we already have.

Stephen has two beautiful children and a loving wife, but suffers from chronic depression because he has debts, and believes he cannot be happy without material wealth. Elizabeth is well off but miserable because she's sure her friends are there only because of her money. Sam, a bright, well-educated 26-year-old, hates his job as a greeting card executive. It's his father's company, but he won't leave because he feels he's not smart enough to do anything else.

Stephen, Elizabeth, and Sam are desperately unhappy. Because they are focusing on what they don't have, they have little appreciation for what's good in their lives.

Does Appreciation Come From Getting What We Want?

A strange fact of life is that most of the time getting what we want won't change the essence of our lives very much. This certainly was true for Michael and Sarah.

Michael and Sarah were celebrating their 15th wedding anniversary with their children, Andy and Michelle… at McDonald's. Michael, a janitor, and Sarah, a secretary, couldn't afford anything better; they were always broke. They constantly fought over money. When they weren't fighting about money, they fought about anything else handy, like the kids, for instance.

Fifteen-year-old Andy recently quit school to "hang" with his home-boys. Michelle, age 14, just announced that she was pregnant. The anniversary dinner quickly deteriorated into a contest over who could scream the loudest at everyone else.

On the way home, Michael stopped at a liquor store for a six-pack and a lotto ticket. Two weeks later this ticket won $6,000,000. For the first time ever, the whole family was ecstatically happy.

****

One year later, they are dining at Ormando's for Michael and Sarah's 16th wedding anniversary.

Michael, now retired, spends his days wandering the rooms of his mansion, drunk. Desperately unhappy, Sarah has had a series of brief, loveless affairs. These include the gardener, the pool boy, her tennis instructor, and, most recently, the UPS man.

Andy was just released from juvenile detention, having served six months for "possession with intent to sell." Michelle is pregnant again. Her boyfriend skipped town as soon as he learned he was about to become a daddy.

Their obscenity-laced expletives lead several patrons to complain. Mustering stern resolve, the Maitre d', for the third time, warns that he will have to eject them if they don't quiet down.

For Michael and Sarah, winning the lottery changed everything... and nothing. They were sure their lives would improve after they won the money. They were filled with appreciation and gratitude over their good fortune. But they quickly adapted to their new circumstances, and, to their great sorrow, found that the essence of their lives hadn't changed at all.

Adaptation, an Equal Opportunity Quasher

> *"Man is a pliant animal, a being*
> *who gets accustomed to anything."*
>
> – Fyodor Dostoyevsky

Adaptation isn't all bad. While it does erode our appreciation for good events, it also reduces the sting coming from bad ones. Listen to Janice's story.

Janice loved horses. She'd been riding since she was six. By age 28 she owned a ranch, 16 thoroughbreds, and was becoming well known as a dressage instructor.

She loved training new horses and was flushed with excitement that fateful Tuesday when she first mounted "Johnny." She was sure that with proper training, this three-year-old could become a champion.

She never sensed disaster lurking as she moved Johnny through his paces. Spooked by the sudden appearance of a snake, Johnny reared, throwing Janice hard to the ground.

On regaining consciousness, Janice was unable to move or feel anything below her waist. The fall had severed her spinal cord and her paralysis was permanent.

Janice was inconsolable. She became profoundly depressed, spending the weeks following her injury in a wheelchair staring out her window. She hardly spoke and had to be coaxed just to eat enough to stay alive.

Four months later, at the insistence of her mother and sister, she agreed to undergo counseling. Shortly thereafter, she began physical therapy. Slowly, the improvement in her body and mind became undeniable.

Although still paralyzed one year later, Janice is back managing her ranch. She is, once again, the cheerful, upbeat person she was before her injury.

Janice's adaptation to her new circumstances was her salvation. We adapt to all circumstances in our lives, the ones we like as well as the ones we don't.

Adaptation Busting

"I get it." Glumbunny says, "I'm always appreciative when I think about it, but it's so easy to forget because I adapt so quickly. How can I stop myself from adapting so I'll be more appreciative?"

"You can't entirely stop adapting, Glumbunny. The best way for you to become more appreciative is by strengthening your conscious awareness, plus learning to live more of your life in the present. We'll talk more about present-moment living in Chapter 14, but you need to understand that you are probably living most of your life in the past and the future; most of us do.

This makes it harder for us to be appreciative.

"Glumbunny, the exercises for strengthening conscious awareness and present-moment living, plus those at the end of this chapter, will help you to be more appreciative."

Appreciation is the Intake, Gratitude the Output

"Gratitude bestows many benefits. It dissolves negative feelings: anger and jealousy melt in its embrace, fear and defensiveness shrink. Gratitude deflates the barriers to love. Gratitude also evokes happiness… "

– Roger Walsh

Appreciation arises when we are fully present to all the wonders that permeate our lives. Once appreciation appears, gratitude will flow naturally and spontaneously. And the more gratitude, the more we will find to appreciate.

Appreciation ←→ Gratitude

As appreciation and gratitude begin playing a greater role in our lives, feedback begins to emerge between them. As we develop more appreciation, this leads to more gratitude, and more gratitude leads to greater appreciation, and on and on.

APPRECIATION/GRATITUDE EXERCISES

Adaptation Busters

<u>Exercise</u>: Although you can't stop adapting to the good things in your life, you can reduce it with greater awareness.

Designate 20-30 minutes every week as "Appreciation time." This is a chance for you to notice and appreciate the miracles you usually take for granted. For instance, one week you might decide to show appreciation for fresh fruit and vegetables:

You could appreciate:
* The grocer who selects, displays, and packages them for you
* The wholesalers who gather the produce early every morning,

transporting them to the grocery stores
* The farmers who till the soil and protect the young plants from disease and insects to produce nutritious crops
* Those who produce the fertilizers that nourish the crops
* The seed and plant producers who supply farmers with healthy plants to grow
* Most of all, the miraculous force of life and diversity contained within the tiny plant seeds

The things about which you could be appreciative are endless. For instance:
* Your friends
* Your automobile
* Your doctor
* Your family
* Your consciousness
* Books
* Your pet
* Christmas
* Television
* Air
* Your birth
* Computers
* Your job
* Electricity
* Chocolate
* Paved roads

Be creative… appreciate things, people, events, anything and everything. Digging deeper into the miracle that is your life will help you minimize adaptation and maximize appreciation.

As you learn to "stop and smell the flowers" through this exercise, appreciation will become a bigger part of who you truly are. The aim of this exercise is to turn appreciation into a habit for you.

Gratitude

Exercise: A daily Gratitude Journal is a simple but powerful way for raising your gratitude consciousness. As with appreciation, you can easily turn gratitude into a habit, a good habit.

Sit down at the end of the day and think of three things you are grateful for that day. List these in your journal.

For instance, Today I am grateful for:

Sunday:
1) Getting an extra hour of sleep this morning.
2) The kids wanting to spend time with me more than they wanted to watch TV.
3) The coffee being especially rich this morning.

Monday:
1) The car starting this morning despite the cold.
2) The boss liking my ideas for the new brochure.
3) Traffic was light so I could get home early.

Tuesday:
1) Having enough that I could give a homeless person a dollar.
2) Having an extra pen with me so I could take notes at the lunch meeting when my first pen ran dry.
3) The clerk at the cleaners being cheerful and friendly.

– and so on –

Be grateful for little things, things like finding a "lucky" penny on the sidewalk, or hearing a child's laughter; anything that brings a smile to your face is a gift. They are all suitable for inclusion in your gratitude journal. The habit of gratitude you'll gain by doing this simple daily exercise can, quite literally, change your life.

Remember, the difference between your appreciation and gratitude journals is that appreciation is a taking-in while gratitude is a sending-out.

******

"Well, this is all well and good," Glumbunny observes, "but appreciation and gratitude just look at the upside of life; what about the downside? What about things in life I <u>don't</u> like, maybe even hate? Too much traffic, bad weather, obnoxious people, money problems, pollution, global warming, world hunger. Is being happy all about finding delight in the good while ignoring the bad?"

"I'm glad you asked about that, Glumbunny. Knowing how to deal with life's upsets, both large or small, is essential to happiness. In the next chapter, Acceptance, we'll look at the relationship between happiness and life's tough stuff."

7

"OH WELL . ACCIDENTS HAPPEN!"

I Never Promised You a Rose Garden

Happiness Key #5: Acceptance

"I accept life unconditionally... Most people ask for happiness on condition. Happiness can only be felt if you don't set any conditions."

– Arthur Rubenstein

"People starving, innocent women and men being slaughtered in senseless war, children terminally ill from preventable diseases; isn't it selfish, maybe even immoral, to be happy while so much misery fills the world?"

This question was asked of me at one of my seminars by Anne, an intense, middle-aged woman. She wasn't trying to badger me, but was clearly distressed by these issues.

How can we be happy when we are surrounded by so much pain and suffering?

Acceptance is the principle that helps us deal with *Sturm und Drang*, the pain of life.

Things We Hate

The last chapter pointed out the importance of appreciating the wonders and delights that illuminate our world. We must now learn how to deal with the undeniable pain that is also there.

We are disturbed when things we don't like <u>happen in the world</u>.

<u>Things like</u>:
* When someone we deplore is elected president
* When our favorite sports team loses a big game
* If the economy stalls and unemployment increases
* If there is a drought in Brazil causing coffee prices to skyrocket
* When water pollution becomes so bad that beaches are closed to public use

We're even more upset when things we <u>really</u> don't like <u>happen in the world</u>:

<u>Things like</u>:
* If a devastating war breaks out in Africa
* When famine brings death and misery to Bangladesh
* When an earthquake in California kills hundreds
* When toxic emissions create holes in the ozone, increasing global warming
* When statistics show the number of people dying from AIDS is increasing

We may become <u>deeply distressed</u> when something we don't like <u>happens to us personally</u>:

<u>Things like</u>:

* When we fight with our spouse or significant other
* When our personal computer gets a virus, wiping out all our files
* If we are demoted at work
* When our best friend insults us
* If we lose a wallet full of money and credit cards
* When the school calls telling us that our son is failing third grade
* If we crash our car in an accident

We may <u>agonize</u> when something <u>really upsetting happens to us</u>:

<u>Things like</u>:
* When a loved one dies
* If our doctor tells us we have cancer
* If we are fired from our job
* If we lose all our money and are forced into bankruptcy
* If an auto accident causes us to lose a leg

"Hey, I thought this is supposed to be a book about happiness?" Glumbunny interjects, "This is pretty depressing stuff. Why do you have to bring this up at all?"

The truth is, there is pain in the world and pretending there isn't won't make it disappear. If you're going to be happy, Glumbunny, you'll need ways for dealing with life's upsets."

"Well, okay, but I don't think there's anything you can say that'll make me like any of the things on your lists."

Pain, Yes; Suffering, No

Glumbunny's right: nothing is going to make us like unpleasant things. But let's see what we can learn from how Glumbunny deals with the disturbing events in his life.

"Glumbunny, tell me about the last time something happened to upset you."

"Sure, that'll be easy. Mmmm, does it have to be something big, major?"

"No, a small example's fine."

"Well, yesterday, on my way to work, this idiot kid in a pick-up truck swerved right in front of me. I had to slam on the brakes or we both could have been killed! I let out a scream and shook my fist at him but he gave me the finger and sped away; I couldn't believe it!

"When I got to work, I couldn't stop shaking, I was so mad. The rest of the day was a waste; I couldn't concentrate. Every time I thought about it I'd get enraged all over again. It still ticks me off, even now. What's wrong with kids nowadays? We're gonna be in big trouble if we can't get these idiots to shape-up."

" Glumbunny, this happened a day and a half ago and you're still upset?"

"You bet! And if I see that juvenile delinquent again I'm going to get his license number and report him to the cops. I have a right to be furious. Everyone at work agreed I was right."

So what's wrong with Glumbunny's reaction? The young man was driving dangerously and was insolent to boot. Glumbunny <u>should</u> be upset, shouldn't he?

There is a Buddhist saying: "Pain is inevitable, suffering is optional."

Being dangerously cut off in traffic caused Glumbunny pain. This pain, by itself, might have lasted three or four minutes, ten minutes at most. All the rest of his upset was suffering generated entirely by his mind. His mind wouldn't let go of what happened, and this gave him an additional <u>35 hours</u> of misery.

Certainly, Glumbunny could justify his suffering; he was right, after all. All his co-workers agreed he was right. But who paid the price? Who suffered? Yes, the price Glumbunny paid for being "right" was more suffering.

And this is just one example of the many upsets we all experience every day of our lives. It's no wonder stress has become the scourge of modern society.

What About Major Pain?

Anne, who earlier raised the question about how to be happy in a world filled with tragedy, is chronically depressed. Let's listen to her some more.

"I can't help being depressed when I see so much suffering in the world. People being slaughtered just because some petty dictator wants to gobble up some desolate piece of his neighbor's land; or ragged children staring hopelessly at the TV cameras begging for a crust of bread.

"I send what little money I can, but I have barely enough to pay my bills. And besides, it never seems to make any difference anyway, the misery just goes on and on. I just feel so hopeless.

"Sometimes I don't even have the energy to get out of bed in the morning."

Anne's reaction may be extreme, but we all hate it when tragedy strikes. How can we be happy, and should we be happy when there is so much misery in the world?

The Serenity Prayer

"God, grant me the serenity
To accept the things I cannot change,
The courage to change the things I can,
And the wisdom to know the difference."

– Rienhold Niebuhr

This amazing little prayer shows us how to be happy in the world despite the ever-present pain.

It teaches that we must accept whatever we cannot change. When fully understood, this wisdom can, quite literally, transform our lives.

We can't change and must accept:
* Bad weather
* Our boss's personality
* Earthquakes
* Volcanic eruptions
* How tall we are
* Sickness
* Aging
* Death

About those things that can be changed, we can choose whether or not we wish to work on improving them.

We can choose to work on:

* Not getting stuck in traffic by avoiding the freeway during rush-hour, or work with local governments to improve traffic
* Reducing global hunger by getting involved with food relief organizations
* Reducing air pollution by working with environmental groups
* Reducing racial, sexual, religious, age, etc., discrimination by working with anti-discrimination groups
* Reducing deaths from preventable diseases by becoming involved with disease prevention organizations
* Reducing illiteracy by volunteering to work with children who have reading problems

Of course, there are many other problems we might choose to change for the better.

The final guidance from the Serenity Prayer, ". . . And the wisdom to know the difference" is vital. We certainly don't want to be like Don Quixote, wasting our energy in fruitless battles with windmills. We want to focus our efforts on those things we can improve.

Can we change what is on this list? Things like:

* Reducing global warming
* Improving human nature
* Ending war for all time
* Getting your boss to lighten-up
* Winning the war on drugs
* Living beyond 200 years of age
* Communicating directly with our spirit or with God

Sometimes it's not easy to know what we can or cannot change. That's why the Serenity Prayer calls it "wisdom."

Why Is There So Much Misery in the World?

"Yes, I see the wisdom in the Serenity Prayer," Glumbunny observes. "Clearly, acceptance is the logical choice to make for those things I can't change. But if the Creator is really the all-knowing, kind, compassionate being or force that I've been led to believe, why are there things like starvation, slaughter of innocent people, and torture? I know I can't get rid of all these terrible things, but it doesn't feel right for me to happily accept them!"

"Of course, you won't **happily** accept terrible things, Glumbunny. However, even sad acceptance of what you can't change will lead to forgiveness and closure. This is the best way for keep those things from blocking your happiness.

"Also, acceptance is more than just logic. Logic placates your thinking mind, but acceptance heals your soul.

"The truth is, none of us knows why things happen the way they do. Of course, that doesn't stop us from judging them. But if we were to be honest with ourselves, we'd have to admit there could be good reasons for everything, even awful, painful things, Divine purpose beyond our understanding.

"So, Glumbunny, we needn't like those things we can't change, but we do need to accept them."

It's hard accepting things like suffering, misery, and death. Having a religious or spiritual background can help, but it's never easy. Nevertheless, understanding that there may be Divine purpose in what we can't change, can help us come to acceptance. The exercises at the end of this chapter will help with acceptance.

Don't Accept Everything

Learning to accept what we cannot change doesn't mean we have to accept everything. We can help make the world a better place by working to improve the things we can change. Doing this well will use every bit of our wisdom, courage, and strength.

Happy people have more energy than their unhappy cousins. People like Anne, whose despair saps their energy, have little left for helping to improve anything.

You can bet the late Mother Theresa, who devoted her life to aiding the poor and sick in the Calcutta slums, didn't waste her precious energy on what she couldn't change. Acceptance allowed her to focus every bit of her strength where it would make the greatest difference.

Would it help the Tibetan people if the Dalai Lama were to roil in hopeless depression due to the unfairness of their occupation and his exile? Or are they better served by him mobilizing the energy generated by his deep inner happiness to spread their message throughout the world?

Living effectively means we need to differentiate between what we can and cannot change. Accepting what we can't change isn't the same as liking or condoning it. But acceptance frees us to put all of our energy and creativity into what we can change and improve. In so doing, we become more effective in the world and promote happiness, for ourselves and others.

ACCEPTANCE EXERCISES

Exercise #1: Identify What You Are Not Accepting.

Take a sheet of paper and title it "What I don't accept." Draw a vertical line down the middle and label one column: "People and things primarily affecting me," and call the other: "People and things affecting the world in general."

Next, place in the appropriate column everything you can think of, trivial to cosmic, that you don't accept. Your lists might look something like this:

People and things primarily affecting me	People and things affecting the world in general
1) My spouse won't quit smoking	1) Global warming
2) I can't get to sleep without pills	*2) Natural disasters like earthquakes, floods, and tidal waves
3) I am twenty pounds over-weight	*3) Bad weather
4) I don't eat enough vegetables	4) Medical Marijuana is still illegal
*5) Someday I'm going to die	5) Slavery still exists in the world
*6) My mother has terminal cancer	6) World hunger

Now, look over each list and place an asterisk (*) before the items you know you can't change. Be realistic about this.

Review the sample lists above. I've placed asterisks before numbers five and six on the left-hand column, and numbers two and three on the right.

Remember, any items on your lists that can't be changed, you'll need to accept. Once again, accepting something is not the same as liking or endorsing it. Acceptance is a tool for helping you put some space between you and what you don't like but can't change. Your energy is limited, so don't waste any of it on what you can't change.

Direct all your effort towards improving the things on your "can change" list.

You'll discover that once you've accepted something, new and better ways for dealing with it will occur to you.

You may have to accept that your mother has terminal cancer, but you could work on becoming closer to her right now. You might speak with her about her life, record her stories, or even produce a written history that would help her grandchildren and great-grandchildren know her as you do.

Examine everything you've marked with an asterisk; these are the things you need to accept.

And you will discover that working on those things you can change will help you better accept the ones you can't change.

Exercise #2: Clearing negative thoughts, feelings and emotions will help lead you to acceptance.

Here's what I do whenever I have trouble accepting something I can't change. I used this technique first many years ago when the University cut my research time by 50 per cent. At the time, it was a heavy blow to my career aspirations, but acceptance led me to something even better, as you'll see in the example below.

But first, find a comfortable place where you will be uninterrupted for 20 to 30 minutes. You'll need to have a notebook and pen for this exercise. At the top of the page record a descriptive title for something that you are currently having trouble accepting, something you can't change and need to accept.

Take several deep breaths, close your eyes and ask yourself:

"What thoughts do I have about (the thing you need to accept)?" Mindfully notice your thoughts. Pay close attention and don't judge or censor anything that comes up. Now, open your eyes and record your thoughts under your title.

Now, close your eyes again and remind yourself that thoughts are neither right or wrong, they're just thoughts. Examine each one without becoming attached to any of them. Don't be drawn into their drama and remember not to judge. Finally, after examining them, let yourself release them, one by one.

When you've finished, open your eyes and look over your list one last time. Then, for each, tell yourself: "I no longer need this thought." Once you've mentally released all of them, physically throw your list away.

Now, take several more deep breaths, close your eyes and ask yourself:

"What emotions am I feeling about (what you need to accept)?"

Once again, mindfully observe every emotion that comes up. When you've finished, open your eyes and record each of your emotions and feelings about what you need to accept.

Repeat the same letting-go process with each emotion just as you did with your thoughts. Mindfully notice and acknowledge each one before letting it go.

Finally, repeat the same process with your fears. Ask yourself, "What fears do I have about (what you need to accept)?"

As with your thoughts and emotions, don't argue with fears. Acknowledge them, give them a full hearing, and then let them go.

Example

Early in my career, my University position was cut by 50 per cent.

Thoughts	"It's not fair"
	"Why me?"
	"They don't appreciate all I've done."
	"How could they do this to me?"
	"I'll be embarrassed when my friends and family find out."
	"What am I to do about this?"
	"I should have gotten an NIH grant like Gil did; they didn't cut his time."
Emotions and Feelings	"I am really angry."
	"I feel so sad."
	"I feel sick to my stomach."
	"I'm scared."
	"I feel like crying."
	"I feel so helpless."
	"I feel vulnerable."
	"I feel threatened."
	"I'm so ashamed."
Fears	"Maybe I'm not smart enough."
	"They really don't like me, I'm too much of a rebel."
	"Now I'll never reach my goal of being a leader in teaching and research."
	"It's a conspiracy, they were just looking for a reason to get rid of me."
	"What ever can I do now?"

Bringing my thoughts, feelings and emotions, and fears into the clear light of my awareness began the inner healing that led me to acceptance. Acceptance freed me to look for new creative ways for working with what I'd been resisting.

Once I accepted the 50% time reduction at the University, I realized that now I had time to develop a teaching program at one of the other hospitals in San Francisco. This turned out to be the best thing that could have happened for my career. Although I couldn't change what had happened at the University, <u>acceptance</u> allowed me to find a creative way to work with my problem.

Now What?

"Glumbunny, do you have any trouble accepting things you can't change?"

"Yes, but it's not my fault. My mother was the big Kahuna in our family. Her word was law. She wouldn't accept anything she didn't like, whether it could be changed or not. I'm that way, too, because of her. I can't help it. It's her fault."

"Things might not be as bad as you believe, Glumbunny, I'm sure that Chapter 8, 'Responsible Adulthood,' will help you out."

8

"SORRY!"

Freedom's Just Another Word for Growing-Up

Happiness Key #6: Responsible Adulthood

> *"The man who makes everything that leads to happiness depend upon himself, and not upon other men, has adopted the very best plan for living happily."*
>
> – Plato

Children, Adults, and Adult Children

When we were young, our parents did almost everything for us. As we grew older and learned to live in the world, we assumed more and more responsibility for ourselves. Most of us have about two decades of apprenticeship before we are expected to mature fully into adults. As adults, we take command over all aspects of our lives... don't we?

> "Glumbunny, how about playing golf with Layne and me, Sunday morning."
>
> "I can't."
>
> "Oh, too bad, how about next Sunday?"
>
> "No, I stay home every Sunday."
>
> "_Every_ Sunday?"
>
> "Yeah, remember I told you how when I was 16 I finally stood up to my mother and refused to go to Church any more?"
>
> "Yes, I remember your saying that."
>
> "I stopped going to Church, but Mom told me if I didn't want to go to Hell, I better stay home and pray. Ever since, I stay home every Sunday. I don't pray but I do repairs, or lawn stuff, or just watch sports on TV, it's not so bad."
>
> "But Glumbunny, you're over forty, you're an adult. _You_ can decide what's right for you."
>
> "Yeah, I know, but I still feel guilty when I don't stay home on Sunday. A couple years ago I went to a neighbor's Sunday barbeque. I had a lousy time because I kept hearing my mother's voice say: 'Why aren't you home thinking about God.' Since then, I stay home every Sunday. Say, why don't you and Layne change your golf day to Saturday?"

Glumbunny's mother died several years ago, but he still lives by her rules. He's a child in an adult's body. Many otherwise bright, accomplished adults live as though they were children.

What Glumbunny does with his Sundays needs to be based on his own decisions. Allowing others to make his life choices for him keeps him from being fully adult.

The late Carlos Castaneda published a series of wisdom books in the '60's and '70's. These books were based on his experiences with the Mexican Indian sorcerer, don Juan Matus. In a memorable passage, Carlos quizzes don Juan about his family and his background. Don Juan startles Carlos by denying he has a family. In fact, he even disavows having a past. Don Juan explains that a warrior, one who fully engages life, must eliminate his personal past history in order to have any chance for success. A warrior must rely entirely on his own inner resources.

Of course, don Juan doesn't mean we have to renounce our families for us to be warriors. Only that *our own inner resources, not forces outside ourselves, must guide and direct our lives if we are to live as warriors.*

Who's in Charge?

"So if I want to be a warrior I have to reject everything my mother said? What about my dad, and my school teachers? Do I have to renounce what they told me too?"

"These are good questions, Glumbunny. No, you don't have to reject anything."

"But you just said I wasn't a real adult because I stay home every Sunday like my mother said."

"You do it because you feel guilty. You didn't freely choose it."

Living as responsible adults doesn't mean we can't learn from others. Parents, teachers, friends, books, newspapers, movies, the Internet, all provide information that can help us. But we need to decide what to accept and what to reject. It's having the freedom to choose for ourselves that matters.

Some people believe that rejecting their parent's values and ideas will set them free. But having not to do or believe something is just as restricting as having to do or believe something.

At some point we must say: "Thanks, Mom. Thanks, Dad. Thanks, teachers. Thanks, everyone for getting me to this point, I'll take over now."

To be fully adult or, as don Juan would say, to be a warrior, means you make the decisions about your life. And living life by your own inner direction is an important key to happiness.

Responsibility for Ourselves

"A secure individual ... knows that the responsibility for anything concerning his life remains with himself—and he accepts that responsibility.

– Harry Browne

It's comforting to cast blame when things don't go our way. "I didn't get the promotion because the <u>boss</u> doesn't like me." "My marriage failed because <u>he</u> was dishonest, immature, and unethical!" "I didn't get the scholarship because <u>the university</u> is prejudiced against ... (Chinese, Blacks, Latinos, women, men, Australians, French, Ukrainians, Vegetarians, etc., etc., etc.)."

Attributing our problems and setbacks to outside forces gives away our power. Life presents us with countless circumstances, some good for us, some bad. It's easy to look with envy to those who already have what we struggle to get. If I toil to make ends meet, I may take my loving family for granted and assume the millionaire "has it made." At the same time, a rich man, mortified by a loveless marriage and predatory children, would trade all his millions for a little love.

In fact, the world is neutral. We all have our mountains to climb. Our problems always seem worse to us than those of others because we see things from our own perspective. Comparing ourselves to others is the height of folly. Each of us has a unique calling. We need to find our purpose and then, with strength and passion, work to <u>fulfill</u> it. This is our own responsibility; no one can do it for us.

Responsibility to Others

Most of what we know about life we learn through trial and error. This means that even with careful planning, our actions may, on occasion, harm others.

Glumbunny orders another glass of Chablis, his third, while his wife, who doesn't drink, fidgets. It's 7:45 Friday night. Marge and Jay were supposed to meet Glumbunny and his wife at Lorenzo's, in San Francisco's theater district, no later than seven. This would allow plenty of time for drinks, a leisurely dinner and good conversation before the short walk to the Curran theater and the 8:30 curtain for "Phantom of the Opera."

"What could have happened to them?", Glumbunny's wife asks, "I hope they didn't have an accident."

"I don't know; it's really getting late, I'm starting to worry too."

"Maybe it's just bad traffic."

"Yeah, but Jay's lived in this area for more than six years. He knows how bad Friday night traffic is.

"Wait, isn't that them now!? Jay, over here!"

Jay and Marge scramble to the table. Their expressions reveal they've been fighting.

"I know we're late," Jay shouts, "but it's not my fault. We left in plenty of time but the traffic was terrible ... I've never seen it so bad."

"Jay," Marge adds, her voice dripping with sarcasm, "it was six-twenty before we left."

"Goddam it, Marge," Jay screams, inches from her nose, "we left at six, sharp!"

"But Jay," Glumbunny says, "you've got to allow at least an hour and a half, on a Friday night. What with the traffic and parking, an hour's not nearly enough!"

"That's just B___S___!" Jay bellows, his face now beet-red. "The traffic's the problem and you're all trying to make me the villain. It's not my fault and you can all go to Hell!"

Noticing everyone in the restaurant watching their drama, Glumbunny's wife says, "Okay, okay, let's just pay the bill and get to the theater, I don't want to miss the curtain."

"So, Glumbunny, how was the show?"

"I have no idea. I'm just glad we got through it without any more fighting."

"And how do you feel about Jay now?"

"I still haven't forgiven him nor has my wife. He's a brat! He still won't admit that he didn't allow enough time. He ruined the evening for everyone."

Jay's first mistake was not allowing enough time to get to the restaurant. But that error was dwarfed by his second, not taking responsibility for the inconvenience he caused others. Instead, he made things worse by insisting he had done nothing wrong and was being blamed unfairly.

> "Glumbunny, once Jay was late, was there anything he could have done to make things better?"
> "Hey, we all make mistakes, I know that. Had he admitted he had done a dumb thing and apologized, I would have forgiven him right away."

Had Jay been contrite, the damage would have been minimal. A sincere apology would satisfy everyone and all would be forgiven. As it is, this minor incident won't be forgotten.

We never want anyone to be harmed by our actions. But when the world surprises us, as it often does, others may suffer as a result. Fortunately, the damage is usually minimal, and heals quickly when we acknowledge our errors and apologize for any harm we may have caused others.

Angry denials and blame-shifting just make everything worse.

Pleasing Others

"Let me listen to me and not to them."

– Gertrude Stein

We can't please everybody; the best we can do is please ourselves. Knowing this brings us one step closer to becoming fully adult. We need to make our own life decisions without undue concern over how others will judge us.

This is not license for reckless behavior. On the contrary, as we take charge of our lives, our responsibility not to harm others increases. This was Jay's error. Knowing we will do everything we can to safeguard others gives us greater freedom to pursue our own goals.

Once we decide upon a course of action, we must disregard both criticism and praise. Proceeding in the face of criticism takes courage, but personal responsibility requires it of us.

> "Hold on," Glumbunny puts in, "I see why it's important to move beyond criticism, but what's wrong with praise? I love being praised."
> "We all like praise, Glumbunny. Enjoy it, but beware not to let your desire for it dictate your actions. It's very easy for us to become addicted to praise. But

those who do quickly lose control over their lives as
they become slaves to their need for it."

RESPONSIBLE ADULTHOOD EXERCISES

Exercise: How many people do you know who are adult-children?
Listen closely to what your friends say when they talk about their
lives and life choices. Especially listen as they speak of their regrets:
the things they wish they'd done, but didn't, or things they did, but
wish they hadn't. What decisions were made based on guilt, or for the
approval or disapproval of others?

You may hear things like:

"Oh, I couldn't do that, what would the neighbors think?"

"Much as I hate doing _____ I do it because I'd feel guilty if I
didn't."

"I'd love to _____, but I wasn't raised that way."

"I always wanted to _____, but my parents wouldn't like it."

"I would be _____, but it would upset my children."

"Personally, I see nothing wrong with _____, but society frowns on
it."

Now ask yourself, how many of your actions or inactions are self-
determined? Do you mostly live by your own inner direction, or are you
controlled by the opinions and judgments of others?

Becoming aware of how much of what you do is influenced by
others will help you regain mastery over your life. Remember, this is
your right as an adult, as a warrior. Base your actions on your own
decisions about what's right for you.

Exercise: Responsibility.

Recall a time when you were hurt by someone who <u>didn't</u> take
responsibility for what they did. How do you feel about what happened?
What are your feelings about the person who caused it? Next, look back
to a time when you were harmed by someone who <u>did</u> take responsibility. In this case, what feelings do you have about what happened and
the person responsible for it?

It's likely that you feel better about what happened when responsibility was taken than when it wasn't. You may even feel closer to those
who took responsibility because you know you can trust them to be
culpable.

Now, recall a time when you were involved in something that
caused upset to someone else. Did you act responsibly? If so, how did

those affected react? How did you feel about yourself? If you didn't act responsibly, what was their reaction? What were your feelings about yourself in this case?

Acting irresponsibly harms everyone, whereas responsible behavior helps everyone feel acknowledged, cared for and safe. Responsibility will help prevent lingering bad feelings, while at the same time promoting healing and closure.

❋ ❋ ❋ ❋ ❋ ❋

"Glumbunny, do you see how important it is for you to be responsible for your actions?"

"Oh, absolutely! One of the managers at work blames everyone but himself when anything goes wrong, even when it's his own fault. I've tried talking to him about it, but he won't listen. He's a jerk! If it were up to me, I'd fire him faster than you could count to one!"

"Glumbunny, this guy really gets to you."

"Well, it's not right for him to get away with it."

"Glumbunny, forget him for a moment and notice how your negative judgment is affecting your mood."

"You're right, I'm gonna be upset for hours."

"You'd better go to the next chapter. It looks at how being judgmental affects happiness."

9

" BAD! DISGUSTING! JUST PLAIN WRONG!"

Just Do It My Way

Happiness Key #7: Non-Judgment

*"Good and bad are judgments about
things in the world, generally based on your
own personal preferences. Those things you
like or agree with, you call good, and the
rest are bad."*

– Wayne Dyer

What's So Bad About Being Judgmental?

Some of the most unhappy people are those who are highly judgmental. Let's look at why this is so.

Judging separates things into dichotomous pairs, right-wrong, good-bad, guilty-innocent, sin-virtue. Judgement fails to recognize shades of grey; everything is seen as either black or white, with nothing in between.

But life is rarely all black or all white, all good or all bad. Almost everything is a blend. When the stock market goes down, it's bad, but not all bad. Many lose money, but buying becomes cheaper. Being laid off is upsetting, but then we are available for other opportunities, maybe something better than what we had. Losing a loved one to illness is devastating, but at least his or her suffering ends.

"Why the puzzled look, Glumbunny?"

"Well, I think I get your point, but I've always believed that one of the most important things we should teach our children is the difference between right and wrong. We've all heard stories of criminals who became that way because they never learned this. Don't we need to judge right from wrong in order to live responsibly?"

"Excellent point, Glumbunny. The great 18th century philosopher, Jacques Rousseau, can help us answer your question."

Help From a Philosopher

"Man is born free, and is everywhere in chains."

– Jacques Rousseau

Early in his life, Rousseau idealized the unshackled primitive. Later, however, he developed and embraced what he called the Social Contract. The Social Contract is an implied agreement whereby individuals subordinate some of their rights, power and freedom for the needs of the community in general.

Listen to his reasoning:

"Man is by nature predominantly good, but he has instincts that must be controlled to make society possible."

Rousseau is telling us that by virtue of being born into society, we have implicitly agreed to follow and obey the laws that are necessary for us to live together. In this case there is right and wrong, and if we break a law we must pay a penalty.

Even here, things are rarely black and white. Just listen to television's "talking-heads" discuss questions of law and you will see how much controversy and disagreement they provoke.

And once we step outside of the legal system, judgment, because it is arbitrary and absolute, is almost never suitable.

> "So, Glumbunny, how judgmental would you say you are?"
>
> "To be honest," Glumbunny says, "I guess I am rather judgmental. I never intended to be like that. How did I become so judgmental, anyway? Oh! One more thing?"
>
> "Sure, Glumbunny, what is it?"
>
> "If you don't mind, could you answer this one without going back to the old philosophers?"
>
> "Okay, Glumbunny, no philosophers this time."

"How Did I Become Judgmental?"

Here are some reasons why so many of us become judgmental.

1) Our authority figures are judgmental. Parents, teachers, principals, police, governmental figures all judged us when we were children. So we grew up believing this is the way we should be when we grow up.

2) Judgments spring from our thoughts and beliefs. We decide how things are supposed to be based on our thoughts and beliefs. This happens even when these thoughts and beliefs are erroneous.

3) Judging is easy. Judgments supply quick, easy answers to almost any question or issue; no need to probe for understanding or more information. Judgment furnishes instant answers about what's good or bad, right or wrong.

4) Judging is habit-forming. Because judgment requires little thought or introspection, it can quickly become a habit.

5) Judging is seductive. Judging produces feelings of superiority. Like the Emperor of Rome, the judge gives final thumbs-up or down to everything and everyone: "That's wrong! He's stupid! That's okay, but barely. That's really dumb! She's pathetic!"

How Judging Kills Happiness

When we're judgmental, we make judgments all day, every day. Most of these judgments will be negative, and negative judgments attract negative emotions like flies to boysenberry syrup. So gradually, under blitzkrieg by their own negative emotions, judgmental people tend to become cynical, pessimistic, and unhappy.

The exercises for this chapter will help us break free of the judgmental habit.

> "Now that you mention it, it does seem like most of the judgmental people I know are grumpy," Glumbunny says. "It makes sense that negative judgments and upsetting emotions go together, but why would you say that most judgments are negative? Why wouldn't just as many be positive?"
>
> "That's true, Glumbunny. I haven't explained that yet."
>
> "Right. Also, since I'm rather judgmental, wouldn't it be easier for me to learn how to make more positive judgments rather than not making them at all? That way, those positive judgments could bring me more <u>happy</u> emotions."
>
> "Glumbunny, I'll show you why most judgments are negative, but I'm afraid I don't know any way for you to make only positive judgments."

Why We Make So Many Negative Judgments

Many of our beliefs come from our thoughts, preferences, and early life influences. Our beliefs tell us how the things and people in our world <u>should be</u>. Judgmental people have very strong ideas about the way everything is supposed to be.

The problem, of course, is that people and the events in the world behave in an infinite number of ways. To the judgmental person, only one way matches his idea of what is right or good. This means all other ways are wrong or bad. So judgmental people inevitably make many more negative than positive judgments.

If Not Judgment, What Then?

"Non-judgment day is near"

– Bumper-sticker slogan

Asking a judgmental person to stop being judgmental will seem to her like she is being told to stop breathing. She's done it so long and so much that she can hardly imagine living without it.

The alternative to judging is evaluating. Judging is easier, less complex than evaluating but much less on-target. We've seen that positive judgment is bestowed only when someone or something closely meets our expectations about how they should be: everything else is "bad" or "wrong." Evaluating requires that we look deeper. We must examine what we are evaluating in detail and create a more complete picture of what we like and what we don't like about it; what is good for us and what is not.

Let's see how Glumbunny, who is judgmental, and Smiley, who favors evaluation, view several news stories in today's paper.

❋ **"President's 19-year-old daughter caught illegally ordering alcoholic beverage."**

Glumbunny: "How embarrassing for the President. Kids today are just no good."

Smiley: "I wonder about that law. Lots of college freshmen experiment with alcohol. They may be holding the President's daughter to a higher standard than other teens. Hopefully this will be a learning experience for her and save her from bigger problems later."

❋ **"Affirmative-action ban revoked by University of California regents."**

Glumbunny: "It's about time. The regents are a bunch of bigots!"

Smiley: "I didn't agree with the ban when they first imposed it. I understand that some of the regents thought affirmative action encouraged reverse discrimination. But it's good to see that a year of peaceful protest has had some effect and that the regents were able to show flexibility."

✳ **"Supreme Court rejects state's medical marijuana initiative."**

> Glumbunny: "Those old fogies on the Court are completely out of touch. They have absolutely no compassion."
>
> Smiley: "I don't agree with this decision. Perhaps they saw that marijuana is listed along with heroin and crack cocaine as a dangerous drug, and that there aren't good medical studies supporting the claimed medicinal benefits. I know studies are going on right now, and if these show benefit, this setback will likely be reversed."

Clearly, Glumbunny's judging is quicker and easier than Smiley's evaluating, but this "benefit" is balanced by its negative tone and off-target simplicity.

Three Cheers for Evaluation

Evaluation is not only more complex than judging, it's also more accurate. The truth is, just about everything has something we can like about it. And when we substitute evaluation for judgment, we will be less polluted by the negative emotions that always accompany negative judgments.

Dropping negative judgments allows us to view everything and everyone as being more interesting and less threatening. Letting go of negative judgments creates a bit of space between us and what happens around us. This helps us see that we are all allies on this incredible journey we call life. We begin to appreciate that life really is a forest, not just trees.

Dropping judgments will help us develop the warm humorous perspective we need for viewing our lives and the lives of others with love and compassion.

NON-JUDGMENT EXERCISES

Exercise #1: Review and question your judgments.

In a notebook, record as many of your judgments as you can recall. Include everything about people and events where you have good/bad, right/wrong judgments. Some may embarrass you, some may be "politically incorrect", but record them all. This exercise is just for you, no need to share your list with anyone else. Take several days to compile this list. Reading the newspaper or watching TV news or talk shows will help reveal your judgments.

Next, examine each judgment closely. If it is a negative judgment, as most will surely be, find something about it that is good, or at least not negative, something your original judgment missed or passed over.

Example

A child is killed by a drunk driver. This is terrible, but often there is some good even in tragedy.

In 1980, after a drunk driver killed her daughter, Wendy Lesko started MADD, Mothers Against Drunk Drivers. Because of MADD, all of our children are safer today. This is an extreme example and it's certainly understandable that we would judge a tragic death to be all bad. Still, the good that came from this catastrophe is undeniable.

Many of your judgments are likely to be arbitrary.

Example

"Kids who cover their bodies with pierces and tattoos are stupid."

You may not like what they're doing, but almost all teenagers go through a period of rebellion. And, like it or not, body piercing and tattoos have been around for millennia.

Evaluating rather than judging would sound something like this: "These kids are rebelling by adorning their bodies. I bet they'll want to get rid of most of them someday when they outgrow their need to shock. When I was their age, I rebelled by becoming an anarchist. At least they're not doing something socially destructive."

Exercise #2: Question new judgments as they arise.

Now that you've examined your current judgments, question each new one as it arises. Look for the errors implicit in their dichotomous nature. Try and catch all of your judgments, and substitute evaluation for each one.

The above exercises will help you replace happiness-destroying judgment with happiness-promoting evaluation.

✳✳✳✳✳✳

"I know I've got a lots to do on this one," Glumbunny says, "I've been judgmental my whole life. But, you're right, my negative judgments are pulling me down. But, whew! I think I need a break. Are any of the happiness keys quick and easy? I'd like one that would raise my happiness right away."

"Glumbunny, I've got just the thing for you. Chapter 10, 'Pollyanna's Game' is fun, easy to learn, and will super-charge your happiness."

10

"OH GOOD—SHE WOULDN'T
BE SO ANGRY IF SHE DIDN'T
LOVE ME!"

Don't Worry, Be Happy

Happiness Key # 8: Pollyanna's Game

*"…the game was to just find some-
thing about everything to be glad about—
no matter what 'twas."*

– Pollyanna

"You're Such a Pollyanna!"

If someone were to say that to us, it would certainly not be meant as a compliment. Pollyanna, the title character in a 1913 novel by Eleanor Hodgman Porter, is the origin of that common pejorative.

Porter's book was an instant success and was soon followed by other "Pollyanna" books as well as a movie in 1920 starring Mary Pickford in the title role.

However, as the years rolled by, the name, "Pollyanna," came to be used for anyone who was <u>inappropriately</u> happy, happy in the face of misery and misfortune. Pollyanna got a bad rap.

Because Pollyanna's Game is such a delightful, not to mention, important happiness principle, it's worth knowing something about its origin.

The Original Pollyanna

As the book opens, Pollyanna's father, pastor of a small mission church out west, has just died. Her mother passed away some years earlier, so the newly orphaned eleven-year-old girl is about to go and live with her well-off but cantankerous aunt in Beldingsville, Vermont.

Three years prior to his death, her father taught Pollyanna the Game that was to bring her, and everyone she touched, joy and happiness. That Game is the inspiration for this chapter.

The "Just Being Glad" Game

A hundred years ago clergymen had no incomes other than what was donated to them by their congregations. Because their parish was a poor one, Pollyanna and her father were forced to live in near poverty.

One day, their Lady's Aid Society sent them a barrel of hand-me-downs. Pollyanna had hoped she might find a doll in this barrel, but sadly, there was no doll. In fact, it held nothing for a child her age but a small pair of crutches. Not surprisingly, she was bitterly disappointed.

Her father, observing her sad tears, decided there and then to teach her the "just being glad" Game. He asked her to try to find something she could be glad about for getting those crutches instead of the doll she wanted.

She tried, she really did, but was unable to think of anything good about getting an old pair of crutches. Finally, he told her: "Why, just be glad because you *don't – need – 'em.*"

That was all she needed for her to embrace the Game; it soon became the core of her life. She especially enjoyed playing the Game when confronted by something really difficult: "And the harder 'tis, the more fun 'tis to get 'em out." And, being dirt-poor, she had plenty of opportunities to hone her skill with the Just Be Glad Game.

But she did discovered that the Game had its limits. "Only – only – sometimes it's almost too hard – like when your father goes to heaven, and there isn't anybody but a Ladies' Aid left."

"Hey! Not So Fast!"

"Wait a minute." a red-faced Glumbunny interjects, "Let's see if I've got this right. I'm supposed to be happy about whatever happens to me, no matter what, except **maybe** if someone I love dies?"

"I might not have put it quite that way, Glumbunny, but, yes, that's right."

"Wha…! Bu…ffaa…! Thaa…that's the most asinine thing I've heard you say yet! If you think … !!"

"Hold on, Glumbunny, don't blow a gasket. I know Pollyanna's Game goes against everything you believe. But if you'll just keep an open mind I'm sure you'll see how it can elevate your happiness."

"Well, okay, I'll go along, for now, but what I really want to tell you is: 'Don't be such a Pollyanna!'"

"Okay, Glumbunny, *touche'*."

Few Things Are <u>All</u> Good or <u>All</u> Bad

"If your house is on fire, warm yourself by it."

–Spanish Proverb

The last chapter showed us that judgment separates things into their polar opposites. However, this separation doesn't represent reality because few things in life are either black or white. Instead, most things are a mix, shades of grey.

Pollyanna's Game recognizes that there is always hidden good in what we consider to be bad. And we can find that good if we just look for it. This understanding, which is the basis of Pollyanna's Game, binds it to reality.

When something happens we don't like, we have three choices: we can try and change it, resign ourselves to it, or we can try and find something about it we can like, something for us "to be glad about."

Notice that Pollyanna's Game doesn't say we must like what we don't like or pretend that black is white. All it asks is that we <u>expand</u> our view of what has happened to include more of what is really there. It is this perspective that shows us how we can find something about almost anything to like.

> "Sorry, I don't buy it."
> "You don't believe Pollyanna's Game will work for you, Glumbunny?"
> "It sounds good but I've already had half a dozen things happen this week that have nothing good about them. No way Pollyanna's Game will work with them."
> "Hm, Glumbunny, would you be willing to put that to the test?"
> "Sure, and lots of luck, you're going to need it."

Glumbunny's "Bad-Stuff" List of the Week

Here is Glumbunny's list:

1) He was cut off on his way to work by a pimply-faced kid who gave him "the finger" when he honked his horn and shook his fist.

2) His wife picked a fight with him, complaining that he was spending too much time at the office and not enough with her or their daughters.

3) Six weeks of dieting didn't change his high cholesterol reading. Now, he's going to have to take expensive medicines that have a long list of possible complications and side effects.

4) He had a fight with the office manager because she insisted on moving him to another office and giving his to a new associate. She justified making the change because Glumbunny's office, being next to her's, would make it easier for her to help the new employee.

5) His accountant just informed him that he has to pay $2000 over his withholding for taxes this year.

6) He just learned that one of his daughters has bulimia which apparently started six weeks ago. She going to need medication and extensive psychotherapy.

"Whew! You've had a tough week, Glumbunny!"

We needn't ignore nor change anything that happens for us to reap the benefits of Pollyanna's Game. All we need to do is search for the gifts that always lie hidden in whatever happens. Generally, when something happens that we don't like, we judge it to be bad and immediately become angry or sad. Pollyanna's Game asks that we withhold our negative judgment and look deeper.

Playing Pollyanna's Game with Glumbunny's Bad-Stuff

1) Being cut off on the way to work upset Glumbunny for more than a week. What's there to be glad about in this? Let's list some possibilities:

✳ No accident or injury resulted from this incident.

✳ The kid knows he upset Glumbunny (he gave him "the finger" when Glumbunny shook his fist) and as he reflects privately on what happened, he might concede his irresponsibility and do better next time.

✳ Even though Glumbunny wasn't at fault, this close call may convince him to drive more defensively, making future accidents less likely.

2) No one enjoys fighting with their spouse. However:

✳ The fight raised issues they need to discuss. Delay would just make a good outcome less likely.

✳ She complained because she wants to spend more time with him. This can only mean that she cares for him and enjoys being with him. Withdrawal would mean she had given up. The fight means she's trying to find a solution.

3) Needing cholesterol-lowering medications is no fun. Still:

✳ Detecting the problem <u>before</u> a heart attack is good. There is still time to prevent serious trouble.

✳ The medicine is expensive but Glumbunny has good insurance. Also, medicine is far less costly and unpleasant than hospitalization for a heart attack or heart failure.

✳ The medicine has potential side effects, but these are known and he will be closely monitored. Should any occur, the medicine can be changed.

4) Changing offices is a nuisance. However:
* His new office might be even nicer than the old one.
* If he hates it, he might be able to change back after the new associate has learned-the-ropes; after all, Glumbunny does have seniority.
* Changing offices gives him a chance to clean out the old clutter that would still be there if not for the change.
* The office manager annoys Glumbunny; now he can enjoy being further away from her.

5) Ugh! Needing to pay an unexpected tax bill is no fun. On the other hand:
* It means he made more money than expected this year. "Good for you, Glumbunny, your hard work paid off!"
* Glumbunny does have the $2000 in the bank; how fortunate that he was wise enough to prepare for this kind of financial emergency.
* This is a good alert for Glumbunny to increase his withholding so he can avoid a tax-bill surprise next year.

6) We hate it when our loved ones have problems. Still:
* The bulimia was caught early, before it became life-threatening.
* Good treatment for the physical and the mental aspects of the disease is available.
* Glumbunny can use this disease as a catalyst to show his daughter how much he loves and supports her. That can bring them closer together.
* The bulimia is a wake-up call for Glumbunny to start paying more attention to all of his loved ones. This disease could be the catalyst for improving all his family relationships.

There are a lot more positives that could be found in the items on Glumbunny's list. That's part of the fun of the Game. Take a few minutes now and find two or three other things Glumbunny could be glad about in these examples. Be realistic. There is no need for fantasy or exaggeration when playing Pollyanna's Game.

Turning Pollyanna's Game into a Habit

"So, Glumbunny, do you understand Pollyanna's Game better now?"

"Yeah. I really do. I'm surprised. Frankly, I expected to hear a lot of wishful thinking. Everything on your list is practical and reasonable. I think I can do this!"

"Thanks for keeping an open mind, Glumbunny. Many people pass off Pollyanna's Game as positive-thinking psychobabble and miss out on one of the simplest but most powerful happiness tools we have."

The more we play Pollyanna's Game, the more skillful we'll be at playing it. The goal here is to turn it into a habit. Once it is, we'll use it automatically when anything we don't like happens.

Remember, Pollyanna's Game doesn't blind us to what is so; we'll be even more connected to reality because we won't be limited to seeing just the negative side of upsets.

What About Pollyanna's Game and Happy Events?

"Hold on," Glumbunny interjects, "I just thought of something. How about when something good happens, something I like? You said Pollyanna's Game works because nothing is all bad, right?"

"Yes, Glumbunny, so ... ?"

"Well, nothing is all good either, right?"

"Absolutely."

"If Pollyanna's Game becomes a habit," he continues, triumphantly, "won't I pull-down my good times by seeing the bad in them?"

Once again, Glumbunny raises a good point. Just as few things in life are all bad, it's also true that few are all good. If we were to use Pollyanna's Game to search for something not to like about our happy events, we'd undoubtedly find them.

"Yes, Glumbunny, you're right, examining favorable events for things to be sad about would certainly uncover things there you didn't like."

"So wouldn't that just balance everything out, the bad become better, but the good become worse?"

"Sure, that's why we use the Game only for finding things to like in unhappy circumstances."

"You can do that?"

"Sure, why not?"

"Oh ... well ... never mind then."

Playing Pollyanna's Game with all our upsets will quickly turn it into a habit. Then, our minds will automatically begin sifting through all our negative events for things to be glad about as they happen.

Happiness Quick-Start

Because Pollyanna's Game is so quick and easy to learn, I call it my happiness quick-start. But don't underestimate its power because of its simplicity. Pollyanna's Game is a very potent, long-lasting way to increase our happiness.

The exercises that follow will help us use Pollyanna's Game to elevate our inner happiness right away.

One caution: Pollyanna's Game is best used for the common, ordinary upsets that plague us day in and day out. Don't use it for major catastrophes. Finding something to be glad about when we suffer major career or financial set-backs, severe illnesses, or when a loved one dies will feel wrong, inappropriate. Remember, Pollyanna herself wasn't able to use it when her father died.

Still, as we develop our expertise we, like Pollyanna, will enjoy using the game even for challenging upsets.

EXERCISES FOR POLLYANNA'S GAME

Exercise #1: Playing Pollyanna's Game with Past Events.

Look back over the last week or two and make a list of all those things you didn't like, things that upset you. Keep going back until you have at least ten items on your list. Skip four or five lines between each item.

Now, let's play Pollyanna's Game. You should have no trouble finding three or four things to be glad about for each one. Reference "Glumbunny's 'Bad-Stuff List of the Week'" if you need help on how to do this. Don't expect to come up with anything that will make you ecstatic; you are, after all, working with your bad-stuff. Finding something modestly good is fine. The benefits are cumulative so, as you continue playing, your happiness will compound.

Exercise #2: Using "The Game" For Current Upsets.

It's easier playing Pollyanna's Game with things from the past because many of the bad feelings have already faded. Although playing the Game for upsets <u>as they happen</u> is harder, it will increase your happiness much more.

When something you don't like happens, your ego-voice immediately will say something like: "Oh, this is terrible!" This immediately opens the door to negative judgments and closes you off to positive alternatives. To use Pollyanna's Game, you will need to fend off your judgments and not allow yourself to be buried under an avalanche of negativity.

In this exercise, as soon as something happens you don't like, ask yourself: "What is there about what just happened that I can be glad about, that I can like?" Don't take time to write anything down, just prompt your mind to begin searching. It will take only a moment or two, but the payoff for your happiness will be tremendous.

If you use Pollyanna's Game for all your upsets, in just three or four weeks it will become a habit. Your friends and family will be amazed at your transformation, but best of all, <u>your happiness will soar</u>.

✳ ✳ ✳ ✳ ✳ ✳

"Glumbunny, you look upset. Are you having problems with Pollyanna's Game?"

"Well, yes and no. Ever since I went over my "Bad-Stuff" list I've been trying to use the Game, as you suggested, as soon as things come up. It works well most of the time, but not all the time."

"Tell me more about when it doesn't work."

"I've discovered that when I've screwed something up, I just can't play the Game."

"Glumbunny, you're not alone. Many of us have trouble accepting our own mistakes. But read on, you'll find lots to help you in the next chapter."

11

"I DIDN'T DO IT, JACK DID
IT... OH, ER, I MEAN IT'S MARY'S
FAULT... OH, THAT IS... I MEAN IT WAS..."

It's Not My Fault; I Can Explain!

Happiness Key #9: Handling Mistakes

*"There are no mistakes. The events
we bring upon ourselves, no matter how
unpleasant, are necessary in order to
learn what we need to learn; whatever
steps we take, they're necessary to reach
the places we've chosen to go."*

– Richard Bach

Early Indoctrination

By the time we are old enough to talk, we learn that we are rewarded when we do things "right" and punished when we do them "wrong." Good behavior, correct performance, wins us love and praise while our mistakes and failures provoke frowns and sometimes even humiliation. Society treats mistakes as sin. It's no wonder that most of us go to such great lengths to avoid making mistakes or the even the appearance of making mistakes.

The brainwashing never stops. Those of us who make the fewest mistakes land the best jobs, earn the most money, and enjoy the greatest acclaim.

Let's, for a moment, visit the mythical kingdom of Right-Wrong where mistakes are regarded as cardinal sins. We've arrived just in time to catch the climax of the annual awards ceremony.

The cherubic herald, wax-sealed envelope clutched tightly in her trembling hand, ceremoniously proclaims to the richly adorned council: "And the Oscar goes to … " she hesitates, nervously tearing at the thick paper binding, "… the winner is … it's a tie! We have a tie! The winners <u>are</u>, Play-It-Safe Nancy and It's-Not-My-Fault George!" The grand old hall trembles as the delegates stomp, scream, and whistle their approval!

Dodging Mistakes

A number of techniques are available for anyone wishing to escape the blame associated with making mistakes. Here are some favorites:

Just Deny It:

"Oh, too bad! Sorry about that, but it's not my fault." "I couldn't help it." "There was nothing I could do."

Denying responsibility for making a mistake is a very simple way for dodging culpability. And when combined with the next technique, The Blame Game, it becomes even more effective. Expert use of the Just Deny It technique is what won It's-Not-My-Fault George, his Oscar.

The Blame Game:

"I didn't do it!" "It's the economy." "It's all the fault of those stupid HMO's." "Patty did it before she left for New York."

The Blame Game is quite popular. It's more complex than simple denial and requires that we find someone or something to blame for our mistake. Best to shift blame to something big and impersonal, or someone defenseless in order to avoid an unpleasant confrontation.

Safe Fortress:

Some arrange their lives so that they won't make many mistakes. This may sound like a good tactic, but it's not.

Safe Fortress people reckon that if they learn all there is to know about one narrow aspect of life, they'll be less likely to make mistakes. However, for this approach to work, they must confine themselves to their designated niche.

Because of extensive knowledge in their subject, they are often deemed to be experts. In reality they are pseudo-experts. Real experts work at the edges of their knowledge. They are constantly challenging the unknown and hence make many mistakes. Real experts do not fear making mistakes.

The difficulty with using Safe Fortress for avoiding mistakes is that inevitably, it leads to boredom and ultimately, desperation.

Still, if the goal is averting mistakes, this tactic works. Play-It-Safe Nancy used her Safe Fortress to perfection in winning her Oscar.

Once More, With Feeling:

Strictly speaking, this is not really a tactic for avoiding mistakes, but it's close enough to include here. Those who use Once More, With Feeling make variations of the same mistake over and over, year after year.

I knew a woman who, after divorcing her husband, went back with him only to, once again, split up. This cycle must have repeated at least a dozen times over the seven years that I knew her. I lost contact with her ten years ago but there's a good chance she's still persisting in her futile pattern.

Those favoring Once More, With Feeling spend so much energy battling their one mistake they have little left to tackle anything else.

When we make the same mistake over and over, we gain the comfort of familiarity, but lose the gift of personal growth that our mistakes can show us.

The critical error common to all these methods is the notion that making mistakes is wrong.

"Wait just a darn minute," Glumbunny interjects, "I'm willing to accept that some good might come from making mistakes, although I'm not entirely convinced, but I fail to see why they deserve praise. A mistake can mess up a project which can cost a fortune to fix. Also, I feel terrible whenever I make one."

"I understand how you feel, Glumbunny, but ... "

"And another thing, it seems to me that with careful planning I ought to be able to do most things without making mistakes."

"Glumbunny, I ... "

"And one more thing, my mother, who was a pretty smart person, always said: 'There's no reason for not getting things right the first time; you don't need to make mistakes.'"

"Okay, okay, Glumbunny, I get that you don't like making mistakes. No one does. Still, if you'll keep an open mind, let me show you how mistakes can teach you valuable lessons."

"Well, okay, as long as I don't have to like making 'em."

How We Learn

"Failure ... is, in a sense, the highway to success, inasmuch as every discovery of what is false leads us to seek earnestly after what is true, and every fresh experience points out some form of error which we shall afterward carefully avoid."

– John Keats

We learn how the world works in many different ways. Let's look briefly at some of the main ones.

Formal Education:
Certainly, school is a major source of learning for us. By first learning what is already known, we can use that information to transport us to the frontiers of knowledge where we can learn even more.

Observing Others:
We glean much by observing how others function in the world, especially those who are successful. This kind of apprenticeship supplements the academic information schools and universities give us.

Research:
Here we hypothesize about how things work and then devise tests to see if we're right, but being right or wrong isn't as important as discovering new knowledge.

Thinking:
Using knowledge we already have, we use our thinking to determine what will work and what won't. Sometimes we're right, sometimes we're wrong.

Intuition:
This is a very powerful path to knowledge, but few of us have developed our intuitive abilities well enough to rely on them. Those who have probably make the fewest mistakes of any of us.

Laboratory of Life:
This is an excellent way for learning about how life on earth works. We learn from both our successes and mistakes. Let''s look closely at this one.

Let He Who Maketh Not Mistakes Cast the First Stone

"The only man who makes no mistakes is the man who never does anything."

– Eleanor Roosevelt

Once formal education is over, most of us lean heavily on thinking when attempting new projects. We think through the steps we hope will lead us to success. We also rely on thinking to anticipate and side-step problems. Thinking leads us to a final action plan which we hope will take us to our goal.

But things don't always go according to plan. Sometimes the unexpected happens: a tool may not be quite right for the job; a worker doesn't perform the way we anticipate; or a critical surprise surfaces halfway though the project.

Despite our planning and thinking, surprises always seem to pop up to confound our best-laid plans.

> "Glumbunny, you're looking perplexed, is something troubling you?"
> "Maybe it's just me, but I am confused. Can you give a concrete example of what you're talking about?"
> "Sure, Glumbunny, that's a good idea."

When I decided to write this book, I had to find a work area, a home office, where I could keep my computer and reference books. I wanted it to be separate from the rest of the house because I write better alone.

There's a little-used room near the front of my house that I reckoned would make a perfect office. I had an old roll-top desk just taking up space where it was. I decided that it would make a fine writing station, so into my new office it went.

When everything was set up, I was dismayed to see a convoy of ugly computer wires and cables coursing awkwardly up and over the top and side of the desk on its way to the printer and power strip. More than just messy, it monopolized a good portion of the desk's work surface.

"Okay," I thought, "I can deal with this." Listen to how my thinking handled this problem.

> "Let's see, how can I get these computer cables where they need to go, neatly and without taking up too much desk space.
> "Hmm, If I were to drill a hole through the back of the desk, the cords could exit through it neatly and efficiently.
> "It's a nice old desk, almost an antique, but it's kinda banged up and would need lots of work were I

to try and restore it. If I ever decide to do that, the wood I want to drill through could easily be replaced. Besides, the hole will be way back, out of sight."

"Let's see ... (rap ... rap) ... it seems to be a very thin board, probably there just for cosmetics. "I'll use my power drill to make the hole, but it'll need to be about twice as wide as it is high. I'll use the one and a quarter inch drill and then widen the hole to three inches by side-grinding with the bit. That'll be plenty large enough for all the cords and fittings to get through."

"Am I forgetting anything? Hmm, nope, I think I've got everything covered."

"Here goes: ...(whirrrrrr ... grrrruuuuu ... KRRUUNNC-Kunk-Kunk-BrruuunK!!-K!!-K!!) ... what the ... OHMAGOD!! Its got a false back! Why would ... ? Ohhh, Good Grief! Of course!! I should have thought of that! The roll-top slides down in there to open and close the desk! I drilled right through the roll-top! I've just trashed my desk! Why didn't I think of that!? And now, with the cables going through the roll top, it won't close anymore! Oh Geeeze!!!"

What happened was a typical left-brain failure, and this by someone some consider to be a reasonably good thinker!

I've discovered that about half the time my plans turn out the way I expect and half the time they don't. I would do as well flipping a coin! Fifty-fifty isn't very good, is it? Still, things aren't as bad as they may seem. Knowing how to handle our mistakes well will be a big help.

Mistakes to the Rescue!

"From their errors and mistakes the wise and good learn wisdom for the future."

– Plutarch

We should look at our mistakes as though they were our teachers showing us what works and what doesn't. But, in order to receive the gifts that accompany mistakes, we must overcome our aversion to making them.

"I knew it! Here comes the pitch. I should *embrace* my mistakes, *love my* mistakes, maybe even throw a meet-my-mistakes party!' I already told you I HATE making mistakes! Even if you prove they're good for me, I'm still gonna HATE 'EM!"

"Hold on, Glumbunny, I'm not asking you to like them. No one enjoys making mistakes. But we can learn more from our mistakes than from our successes. If you want to live your life effectively and happily, you're going to need to learn how to use mistakes, like 'em or not."

"Well, all right, but why can't I learn as much from getting things right the first time, like my mother said?"

Glumbunny has a point: we can learn from successes. When we plan action that goes well, we learn. However, success just confirms what we'd already figured out so it can't move us very far forward.

But when something <u>doesn't</u> go the way we expected, we have a chance to learn something we didn't know before. Our mistakes give us new information about the world, ourselves, and how we can act more effectively in the world. This is not theory, not concept or belief; this is real action in the laboratory of life! Mistakes show us the errors in our thinking, and then give us clues about how to fix those errors.

"I don't buy that," Glumbunny interrupts. "Lots of times things don't work even when I know I've done everything right. For example, two months ago I missed a connecting flight in Dallas because my incoming flight was delayed 45 minutes. That wasn't <u>my</u> fault.

"Also, last week I'd arranged to meet a potential client for lunch at Max's. I waited and waited but he never showed. Turns out, there's another Max's in the suburbs and he went there. That's an hour from the office, he should have known to go to Max's downtown. He screwed up, not me. But he got mad and I lost the account even though it was <u>his</u> fault."

"Gee, Glumbunny, maybe It's-Not-My-Fault George should share his Oscar with you."

How to Learn From Mistakes

Our mistakes <u>always</u> carry powerful lessons for us. Understanding this makes it easier for us to learn what we need to do differently so we can be more effective the next time.

Let me be clear: this is not an excuse for crying over spilt milk. The trick is to learn the lessons from our mistakes **the first time**! Doing this means we won't have to repeat them. We can go on and make new mistakes, thereby learning new lessons about ourselves and how we operate in the world. Then, bit-by-bit, we will become progressively wiser and wiser.

Remember how I used mistakes to guide me to inner happiness? Knowing what <u>didn't</u> work, and refusing to repeat those errors, led me to eventually discover what <u>did</u> work.

Here are the keys that will help us use our mistakes for becoming wiser and happier. Welcome your mistakes for the life-lessons they hold. You needn't like or enjoy making mistakes, few of us do. Do everything possible to avoid them, but if you're "out there" in the world, mistakes will find you. Whenever it feels to me like I'm not making enough mistakes, I check to see whether or not I'm <u>playing it too safe</u>. It may be time for me to reach out more boldly into life's wonderful testing ground.

Also, learn the lessons from each of your mistakes <u>the first time</u>. Don't compete with Play-It-Safe Nancy or It's-Not-My-Fault George. Owning-up to your mistakes is the only way to receive their gifts. Learning from your mistakes right away moves you quickly on to new mistakes where you will learn still more…

Using mistakes like this means that as time goes by you won't just grow older, you'll become wiser as well; and happier too.

EXERCISES FOR HANDLING MISTAKES

<u>Exercise #1</u>: Review and Claim Your Past Mistakes.

Think back over the past few weeks and months and find examples of things you planned that went wrong. They needn't be big things; small examples of negative outcomes are fine: a meeting with a colleague that didn't go well; an argument with a family member; a trip-planning mishap; a repair project that went bad; a decision that caused you to lose money; any negative outcome will do.

Record four or five of these in a notebook, one to a page.

Now, examine each negative outcome and find at least one mistake you made that contributed to what went wrong. Don't be defensive; open up to your mistakes. Then record all of your mistakes in your notebook.

Finally, find the learning your mistakes have for you.

Let's use Glumbunny's examples as our model:

1) <u>Negative Outcome</u>: Glumbunny missed a connection because his initial flight was unexpectedly delayed.

<u>Mistake</u>: Flights are often delayed. We need to anticipate this and build an allowance or cushion into our travel plans.

<u>Learning</u>: Next time, anticipate common travel problems like unexpected delays. Schedule more time between connecting flights. Waiting a bit longer in an airport is preferable to missing a flight. And while you're at it, anticipate other common flying problems like errant baggage. Always use carry-ons when possible. If not, at least keep essentials like key notes for a meeting, in your carry-on.

2) <u>Negative Outcome</u>: Glumbunny missed an important lunch meeting with a potential client when they went to different restaurants.

<u>Mistake</u>: Glumbunny wasn't clear enough with his potential client about where they were to meet for lunch.

<u>Learning</u>: Arrangements for meetings with others need to be specific, complete, and unambiguous. Be sure all parties know the day, date, hour (including AM vs. PM), place, address, and where to meet (e.g., at the bar, at the cashier's counter, at the table (reserved under whose name?). Also, what to do if something unexpected happens; e.g.: a flat tire, terrible traffic, some office or personal emergency, etc. A cell phone is a big help for handling the unexpected.

Exercise #2: Learning from Current Mistakes.
Start a new notebook and label it "Lessons from my mistakes." In this notebook record your mistakes as they happen. As in exercise #1, first record the negative outcome, then your mistakes, and finally note the learning your mistakes brought you.
If you're like most people, it may take a while for you to acknowledge your mistakes. If so, just record the negative outcome and wait until you recognize your part in it. This will be easy once the pain from the negative outcome begins to fade. Then document your mistakes and look for and record the lessons there for you.
As you continue with this exercise, recognizing your mistakes will become less painful and your learning will accelerate. Eventually, handling mistakes to maximize your learning will become a habit, a good habit, and your wisdom and happiness will grow.

* * * * * *

"I have to admit," Glumbunny notes, "this is a new way for me to look at mistakes. It would be great if they could actually help me. I wonder," he said thoughtfully, "if I could use mistakes to help me become a better person? Maybe I could become really creative at work instead of being a plodder; or perhaps become a charming extrovert at parties, always making clever comments that impress everyone, instead of being a boring introvert. My mother always wanted me to be creative and dynamic. Could I fix any of that using this new approach?"

"Maybe, maybe not, Glumbunny, but trying to change who you are may not be the real problem. The next chapter, 'I Just Gotta Be Me,' will help answer your questions."

12

"I'll just take the road less traveled!"

I Just Gotta Be Me

Happiness Key #10: Individuality

> *"If a man does not keep pace with his companions, perhaps it is because he hears a different drummer. Let him step to the music which he hears, however measured and far away."*

> – Henry David Thoreau

So what's wrong with trying to be the person others want us to be, especially when we know they have our best interests at heart? Why shouldn't Glumbunny try to "fix" himself in order to become more like what his mother wished him to be? From the moment we're born, parents, teachers, clergy, role models all try to turn us into ideal little boys and girls. What's so bad about that? And as we mature into adults, society does its best to shape us into model citizens. What's wrong with that?

Well, it's a bit like Chinese foot-binding. Believing tiny feet to be a reflection of feminine beauty, ancient Chinese culture encouraged parents to bind their daughters' feet to keep them child-sized. This practice, now thankfully ended, produced painful, permanent deformities that crippled countless women.

Similarly, when we allow our personal growth and development to be bound by someone else's concept of virtue, no matter how well meaning, we'll be damaged. We can learn to be effective and ethical in the world without losing our individuality. We all have genius within us related to our unique qualities. But for most of us, discovering that genius means we must find the courage to overcome the tremendous pressures society exerts upon us to conform to its ideal of what's normal and right.

Why All This Pressure to Conform?

"Yes, Glumbunny, you have a question?"

"I get your point, but people who flaunt the rules are criticized, sometimes even ostracized. I've taught my daughters that it's important for them to fit in, to follow the rules. I've tried to prepare them for living the right way in our society. Are you telling me that I shouldn't be doing this?"

The answer to Glumbunny's question is: "It depends." If our main goal is for our children to grow into compliant adults who follow the rules and don't make waves, then it makes sense to stifle their unique qualities.

Furthermore, it's much easier for a society to govern when its subjects don't stray very far from the norm. In that sense, we can certainly understand why, throughout the ages, governments have wanted their citizens to be homogeneous.

Schools and businesses also find it easier to deal with a uniform student body and work force rather than a collection of iconoclasts.

Primitive cultures were always suspicious of outsiders, fearing conquest, slavery, and loss of tribal identity. This is reflected today in our distrust of anyone who stands apart from the group. We may be fascinated by, or even attracted to, those who are different, but ultimately we reject them.

"Yes!" Glumbunny trumpets excitedly, "Precisely my point! I don't want my girls to be excluded. Heck, I don't want to be set apart from others, either. This time I got it right! Come on! Admit I'm right."

"Glumbunny, I'd love to agree, I know how much you like being right. But remember, I said 'it depends' when you asked about raising you children to conform. Let me tell you what else it depends on before you celebrate."

"I should have known there was a catch. Okay, fine, what else does it depend on?"

The Price Tag For Conformity

"Nobody is so miserable as he who longs to be someone other than the person he is."

– Angelo Patri

The message most of us are taught by our parents, teachers, and the rest of society is that we are not okay the way we are; we need fixing. But we pay a big price for allowing others to decide how we should be. Let's look at some of these costs.

Costs of conformity:

Conformity can lead us to:

* Feelings of low self-esteem
* Feelings of low self-love
* The belief that something is wrong with us
* Feelings of self-alienation
* Difficulty in trusting ourselves
* Feeling that we don't know who we are
* Difficulty relating honestly with others
* Feeling that we don't fit in
* Being unable to find and use our greatest gifts while working in the world
* Being more susceptible to job dissatisfaction and early burn out
* Feeling resentful and rebellious and blaming others for our discontent

* Intolerance for the nonconformity of others

This list could go on and on. Suppressing who we are forces us to spend an enormous amount of energy maintaining our confinement.

The final item on this list, intolerance for the nonconformity of others, I find to be particularly interesting. It's as if a prisoner gazing through his jailhouse bars spots someone outside, enjoying freedom. But rather than wishing freedom for himself, he wants to imprison the free one.

"Let None Be Free!"

"I have observed that society in general always seems to honor its living conformists and its dead troublemakers."

– Wayne Dyer

Just like the prisoner, society manifests little tolerance for those who stray very far from what the group considers to be normal. Yet, as author Wayne Dyer points out, we have nonconformists to thank for much of our human progress. Refusing to suppress their individuality, their genius was freed to benefit the very society that criticized and ridiculed them.

Television talk shows provide living demonstrations of this tribal rejection in action. Watch one that features guests who do out of the ordinary things. Perhaps a young person living in a commune, or a mother who chooses to home-school her children, or maybe a couple where the wife is the breadwinner and the husband keeps house. Favorite targets are those who have the audacity to follow unusual religious or spiritual practices.

Invariably, the audience is disapproving, often screaming insults at these sacrificial guests. This is so even when it is clear that what they are doing harms no one. The outrage is simply because these guests are doing something different from what is considered to be normal behavior.

"Let's see if I've got this straight." Glumbunny murmurs. "If I yield to social pressure and conform, I'll lower my self-love and esteem, develop self-alienation, as well as all those other unpleasant things on your list. On the other hand, if I resist and remain true to myself, I'll be disdained by my tribe, maybe even run out of town. Have I got that right?"

"Glumbunny, it's nice to know how carefully you've been listening. I admit it sounds bad, but keep reading; help is on the way."

Individuality; Is It Really Worth the Struggle?

"If you obey all the rules you miss all the fun."

–Katherine Hepburn

Why is it so important for us to insist upon being who we are? Let's look at some of the gifts that individuality brings.

Benefits of Individuality:

When we live true to who we are:

* We have higher self-esteem, self-love, and self-acceptance
* We are more willing to trust ourselves
* We can relate more honestly and deeply to others
* We are better able to connect with our greatest abilities, our genius
* We are better equipped to find work we love
* We will have less stress and greater life satisfaction
* We will have greater fulfillment and happiness
* Ironically, others will give us more acceptance and esteem
* We have greater appreciation and acceptance for others who choose to be true to their individuality

Who, of all your friends and acquaintances, do you most admire? Of all those alive in the world today, who are those you hold in highest esteem? And which people throughout all of human history, do you most highly regard? I suspect the majority of those on you're lists are people who insisted on maintaining their unique individuality. It's interesting, isn't it, how often our greatest role-models are those who most resist the pressure of conformity?

Toning-It-Down

At the beginning of this book I told the story of how my colleagues were upset by my open display of happiness. It seemed that expressing too much happiness, without good reason, was too much for my tribe to accept. What should I have done? Should I have stifled my happiness? Of course not! In this case the solution was obvious; I just toned down my <u>outer</u> expression of happiness. Inside, I was as happy as ever.

Toning-it-down doesn't require that we pretend to be someone or something we're not. It's usually quite easy to sense how far we can go without attracting tribal censor. And certainly, we will still express every bit of our individuality to trusted friends, family, lovers and, most importantly, to ourselves. Toning-it-down is a simple but powerful tactic we can use for fitting into society, while at the same time, remaining true to who we are.

Although toning-it-down is effective, it's not very exciting. There's another way to accomplish the same thing that's lots more fun. This other way, I call, the Eccentricity-Gambit. But be warned, using the Gambit can be risky and requires lots of skill for it to be effective.

The Eccentricity-Gambit

Our society, or tribe, has left a small space called "eccentric" located between normal and what it thinks of as crazy. Those who are comfortable with their individuality will just naturally find their way to eccentricity. Being identified by our tribe as an eccentric accords us many rewards.

<u>Eccentricity's Gifts</u>:

* Society gives eccentrics permission to be authentically who they are without exclusion or punishment.

* Society considers eccentrics to be highly intelligent and unusually gifted. Ordinary people believe eccentrics see things they can't. This is because eccentrics are allowed to be more open in expressing their individuality than are other members of the tribe.

* Eccentrics are sought-after guests at parties, and their opinions are highly valued by others. This is because they are regarded as being unusually interesting and creative.

* Mistakes made by eccentrics are not held against them. It's assumed that their mistakes are an integral part of their unique creative process.

Eccentrics are embraced as valued members of their tribe even as they are permitted the freedom to be who they are. So why isn't the Eccentricity-Gambit for everyone? Because, if we don't play it skillfully, we run the risk of being called crazy by society. And being labeled as crazy is never good.

Taken too far, the Eccentricity Gambit will quickly deliver us across the line into crazy. Understand that "crazy," as used here, doesn't imply a psychiatric diagnosis. Society considers anyone who acts too differently from others to be crazy. So, it's important that when using the Eccentricity-Gambit, we tone-it-down enough to avoid being considered crazy. This is an art requiring us to know exactly where the line is that separates eccentric from crazy.

> "I think, for me," Glumbunny intones, "your Eccentricity-Gambit has crossed the line into crazy. I can't believe I have to play such stupid games just to be myself."
>
> "I know it sounds like I'm trivializing, but the fact is that we are under tremendous social pressure to conform. Toning-it-down and the Eccentricity-Gambit may sound silly, but they are both powerful, proven tools for helping us maintain our individuality."
>
> "Hmm, maybe what I need right now is for you to illustrate a real-life example of the eccentricity-gambit."
>
> "That's an excellent suggestion, Glumbunny."

Most of those who enjoy the benefits of eccentricity arrived there by accident. They simply refused to suppress their individuality. They hadn't set out to become eccentric. This was certainly true for me. My life was falling apart in 1970. My marriage was over and I realized my old way of living wasn't working anymore. It was despair that gave me the determination and courage to insist on being exactly who I was.

Tie or No Tie, That Is the Question

> I was a junior member of a very prestigious research foundation in 1970. Including a year of fellowship, I had been there a total of four years.

The Foundation had a clear though unofficial male dress code: sports jacket, slacks, dress shirt, and necktie.

I **hated** wearing neckties! With my life falling apart all around me, I decided the heck with the rules; I was going to be true to myself, dammit! So, one Monday morning I arrived at work without a necktie. Although afraid that I'd be severely reprimanded, at best, maybe even fired, all my tie-less rebellion brought were a few funny looks and humorous comments from my colleagues and superiors.

Surprisingly, this rebellion was not just accepted, but also brought me greater acceptance and personal freedom than anyone else there.

Encouraged, I soon shucked the sports jacket and even let my hair to grow a few inches longer than was standard for members of the Foundation.

This behavior was enough to earn me permanent eccentric status.

While discarding one's necktie might not seem like a very radical deviation from the norm, in this setting, it was. Achieving eccentric status won me greater freedom for expressing my individuality. If anything, my work and opinions were even more respected than before I was granted eccentric status at the Foundation.

How to Use the Eccentricity-Gambit

In order for the Eccentricity-Gambit to work we must learn the rules for the group in which we're using it. Knowing the rules enables us to gently bend them. Anyone who rides roughshod over tribal rules risks crossing the line into crazy. The punishment for carrying this "Scarlet letter" may be virtual exclusion from society.

Next, it's important that we be functioning within the group at a high level. I knew my work at the Foundation was solid. Marginal members of any group who attempt the Gambit may be seen as trouble-makers and will be quickly dismissed if they try to bend the rules.

In whatever way we choose to express our individuality, we should be careful to do no harm. Also, we should launch only those changes that are important to us. Harmful or trivial violations of tribal rules will not usually be tolerated, nor should they be.

The Eccentricity-Gambit is not for everyone. It requires a great deal of sensitivity and awareness to pull it off. It's always best to tread lightly and not attempt too much too soon. Anyone to whom this feels artificial, manipulative or silly, would be best advised to just use toning-it-down for maintaining their individuality.

INDIVIDUALITY EXERCISES

Exercise #1: Who Are You?

How can you be who you are without knowing who you are? After conforming to years of parental and societal influences, discovering your individuality will take time and effort. A reliable guide is to heed the late Joseph Campbell's urging to "follow your bliss."

Imagine your life to be a laboratory. Carry a small notebook with you and jot down everything that happens during the day that brings you special joy or excitement. This might be an event, an idea, or even something from your senses.

Do the same for anything you find to be especially upsetting. A small thing that leads to an emotional reaction out of proportion to the event itself is often your best clue.

Record both blissful and upsetting episodes in separate columns. Following your bliss, and anti-bliss, can teach you a lot about who you really are. Why did you react as you did? How did you feel about what happened? Especially note surprises that pop-up in either list.

Example

Bliss: 1) "On the way to work I noticed two squirrels having a great time chasing each other. I felt close to nature and that filled me with overwhelming joy." (Maybe nature and simple pleasures are important for you.)

2) "At work, I helped Jane fix a couple of sentences in her quarterly report. She was very appreciative; I still felt great about it hours later." (Maybe helping others is an important part of your nature.)

Upset: 1) "I was furious when I saw gopher mounds on my lawn." (Maybe maintaining order is important to you.)

2) "It really got to me when Joe left his coffee cup and cookie crumbs for someone else to clean up after his break." (Maybe responsibility is an important value for you.)

Repeated patterns and strong reactions in this exercise provide you with good clues for discovering your individuality.

Exercise #2: Toning-it-down.

As you expose your individuality, you will probably uncover aspects of yourself that go beyond society's narrow range of normal. While you expect your close friends to love and accept who you truly are, some toning-it-down may be necessary for casual acquaintances or co-workers.

Example

When I saw how annoyed my colleagues became by my expression of happiness, I just toned-it-down a bit. Now, when someone at work asks how I am, I smile and say "Great!", but I don't go into detail about the wonders of life and how fortunate we are to be living on this incredible planet. I save that for good friends whom I've chosen, in part, because they enjoy my optimism and enthusiasm.

Exercise #3: Playing the Eccentricity-Gambit (Optional)

This is optional because many of you will find the Eccentricity-Gambit too risky and too attention-getting for your tastes. It's best used only after you've learned to accept your individuality and decide how best to express it with others.

Rules for Using the Eccentricity-Gambit

1) Decide which part of your unique character you wish to express.
2) Decide where you wish to express it (at work, on the golf course, everywhere, etc.)
3) Construct an Eccentricity-Gambit plan of action:
    * What is the nature of the group (work, club, church, etc.)?
    * What are the rules and limits of the group (dress code, politics, etc.)?
    * Who are the key individuals in this group?
    * How much eccentricity and what kind would be acceptable?
    * What behavior in this group would cross the line into crazy?
    * Plan action that expresses your individuality but is in no danger of crossing the crazy-line for this group.
    * Be sure that your action will harm no one.
    * Initiate your action and then evaluate how it was received.

  ✳ If all goes well, cautiously move forward to complete
    the Gambit.

A close friend or ally can help, but only you can decide how far to
go with your Eccentricity-Gambit. Remember, if things start to become
problematic, you can always simply revert to toning-it-down.

Refer to my no-tie, no-jacket, long-hair example of how to use and
develop the eccentricity-gambit.

✳ ✳ ✳ ✳ ✳ ✳

"Toning-it-down makes a lot of sense to me, but I
don't know if I'll ever be ready for the Eccentricity-Gambit."

"That's fine, Glumbunny, it's an option; it's not for
everyone."

"Anyway, I'm not so sure I'd want a bunch of stran-
gers to know how imperfect I am. What I really need is
to figure out how to fix my deficiencies."

"Glumbunny, maybe what you need most is to see
yourself in a better light."

"But I know how flawed I am. Just the other day I
was thinking about how there isn't a single thing about
me that's perfect, and there probably never will be."

"You are so ready for the next chapter, Glumbunny;
you have a lot to learn about perfection."

"AHHH... PERFECT, JUST AS WE ARE!"

Who Says Nobody's Perfect?

Happiness Key #11: Perfection

"The year's at the spring and the day's at the morn; morning's at seven' the hillside's dew-pearled; the lark's on the wing; the snail's on the thorn; God's in His heaven – all's right with the world."

– Robert Browning

The dictionary defines "perfect" as: "Conforming absolutely to the description or definition of an ideal type: a *perfect* gentleman," and "excellent or complete beyond practical or theoretical improvement."

Most of us know that it's not possible for us, or anyone else, for that matter, to be entirely perfect at anything. We've known since we were children that we were loaded with imperfections. Our parents were quick to point out how often we did things wrong and how much better we could be than we were. At school, they even scored our imperfections alphanumerically: "Frank, you got a 73, a C-; Mary, 88, that's a B+; and, oh, my, Johnny, only a 43, that's an F. What's wrong with you, Johnny, you can do better than that."

Imperfect Us

Growing up didn't help much. No matter how good we were at anything, there was always someone better. We may say to ourselves: "My tennis game's not bad, but Roger beats me every time." or "My backhand is strong, but I have a weak serve." or "I am a good medical investigator, but I still make mistakes." "I'm a good speaker but, there are always some in the audience I can't reach." "My writing's improving, still not flawless."

"You Are Perfect, Perfect Just As You Are."

The date, February 1970, the place, San Francisco's old Jack Tar Hotel, the event, the Erhard Seminars Training (EST).

I was 36 years old and my world lay in devastation. My marriage of 14 years was over and I was seriously thinking of quitting my promising medical career. And, perhaps worst of all, I discovered that I had no idea who I was. Not surprisingly, I was disappointed, angry, and bitterly unhappy.

Werner Erhard had begun offering the EST training seminars several months earlier. I signed up, desperate to find my identity and hoping to get a new start in life.

The EST seminars attracted lots of attention in San Francisco for two reasons. First, they were purported to be remarkably effective for changing peoples' lives, and second, no bathroom breaks were allowed during any of the four-hour sessions.

My timing for taking the EST training was ideal. My old life was in ruins and EST gave me the basis I needed for a new start. But there was one concept, try as I may, I could not fathom: the notion of perfection.

Although thirty years have passed, I still vividly recall Werner, prowling the stage, resplendent in his immaculately pressed, powder-blue slacks and crisp white sports shirt, open at the neck, thundering: "You are all perfect, perfect just as you are!" Then, altering the wording for emphasis, he repeated this mantra half a dozen times more to be sure we "got it."

I, along with the 250 other attendees, roared in sycophantic agreement, all the while thinking: "Perfect? You've gotta be kidding. I'm far from perfect! Oh, I'm above average in some things, but not perfect. I'm mediocre in many more areas and downright lousy in others. But perfect? No way!"

"Exactly," shouts a beaming Glumbunny, "nobody's perfect. I love it when you make my points for me. Perfection isn't possible for any of us. Is that your point, no one's perfect?"

"Glumbunny, my answer has to be both yes and no."

"What a wishy-washy answer! Why can't you just say 'yes'? You know that no one's perfect. Why won't you just say so?"

"Glumbunny, let me explain my answer."

"Okay, okay," he says, resigned, "explain."

Glumbunny's Right, Nobody's Perfect

"Perfection does not exist. To understand this is the triumph of human intelligence; to expect to possess it is the most dangerous kind of madness."

– Alfred de Musset

Perfection, in whatever we undertake, is not humanly possible. We all know this. Trying to prove it would be a waste of time. Still, it's one thing to know something in our intellect and quite another to know it in our gut. We all know perfectionists, people who obsess over every detail of what they do and take twice as long as anyone else to do it. But even perfectionists admit that nothing they do is really perfect. Still, most of us feel we should be perfect.

We are constantly comparing ourselves unfavorably with others. John rebukes himself because Francine is better than he at math. The fact that he gets along with people better than she doesn't comfort him. Because Layne's golfing short-game is superior to mine, I feel inferior even though my long-game is better than his. These kinds of comparisons highlight our imperfections making us feel as though we're failures.

Holding ourselves to arbitrary standards is another way of highlighting our imperfections. These standards, mostly socially-constructed ideals, set impossibly rigid codes of conduct for us to meet. Let's look at some of them.

To be perfect, we believe we:
* Must never tell lies
* Should exercise five times a week
* Must not eat junk-food
* Must drink alcohol only in moderation
* Shouldn't waste time
* Should always balance our checkbooks
* Should go to church every week
* Shouldn't harbor bad thoughts about anybody
* Mustn't use cuss-words
* Shouldn't gossip
* Shouldn't procrastinate
* Should pick-up after ourselves

Society's standards let us know what we must do to be perfect. Even though many admirable things are included in these standards, their rigid call to perfection is oppressively inhuman.

Trying to meet society's ideals for perfection is not humanly possible. Still, many of us try to do just that. And our inevitable failure leads us to feelings of inadequacy and guilt.

"So, yes, Glumbunny, not only is it impossible for us to be perfect, but we'd be foolish to try."

Glumbunny's Wrong, We Are All Perfect

*"Be ye therefore perfect, even as
your Father which is in Heaven is perfect."*

–Matthew

Many religious and spiritual traditions speak of human perfection. Most of us assume this is meant metaphorically or reflects biblical exaggeration. This was my reasoning as Werner, eyes wide, foam spraying from his lips, thundered, "YOU ARE ALL PERFECT!" Still, I wasn't entirely comfortable with this ethereal assessment since everything else about the EST program had been so practical, so down-to-earth.

It took ten years for me to understand Werner's meaning about perfection. It happened early in my relationship with Jillian when she came to see me one evening in tears.

Jillian had been working as a legal word-processor for a little more than two years. In the beginning, her relationships with the partners and her coworkers had been genial. However, for the last two months, things had become decidedly less copasetic. She had several unpleasant run-ins with a secretary and one of the junior attorneys had taken a dislike to her.

When everything came to a head that afternoon, she left work early, both frightened and angry.

Sitting on the edge of the bed still dressed in her tailored blue work-suit, she detailed the injustices she had endured that day. She was sure she would be fired.

It was the mid-80's and Jillian had already taught me the value of supportive listening. To simply listen, not make suggestions, not "fix" anything, just be there with her, listening.

When the tears started, my attention was drawn to the black trails of mascara coursing down both her cheeks like snail-trails. Her eyes puffy and red, nose running, she relived every detail of her bedeviled day.

As I sat there, just being with her, it occurred to me that instead of finding her sad-angry disarray unattractive, I found that it enhanced and confirmed her beauty and authenticity. In a flash of insight, I realized I was, in that moment, witness to perfection: Jillian's perfection at quite simply being Jillian. No amount of sadness, no quantity of mascara-mess, in fact, nothing could detract from Jillian's unique perfection.

In that magical moment I understood that we really are perfect, all of us, all the time, effortlessly. If a great actress were to portray Jillian in a dramatic performance, even with an unlimited budget, unlimited time, and unlimited talent, she could never be anything but a flawed imitation of the real thing. Only Jillian could be <u>perfect</u> at being Jillian!

Being the Best Me I Can Be

Werner was right, we <u>are</u> perfect, perfect just as we are. It's built into us. We can't be anything but perfect no matter what we do and no matter what happens to us. This is spiritual perfection and nothing like the impossible, arbitrary, artificial perfection posited by society.

All of us embody spiritual perfection. We need do nothing different to have it and it can never be taken from us.

> "So, if I'm spiritually perfect right now," Glumbunny offers, "and so is everyone else, why would I be motivated to improve? Why would anyone? Maybe I should just quit my job, leave my family, and spend every day drinking beer in front of the TV? I'd still be perfect, right?"
>
> "Sure, Glumbunny, you would be perfect as Glumbunny doing those things. Is that what you want to do?"
>
> "No, of course not."
>
> "Even though you'd still be perfect?"
>
> "No."
>
> "Why not?"
>
> "I wouldn't want to waste my life and hurt my family and myself like that."

Accepting that we are perfect won't make us irresponsible nor will it stop us from doing what we can to improve ourselves. Glumbunny is perfect at being who he is. And if he wants to learn some new skill, then he will. Developing new abilities, improving himself, or even becoming happier won't affect his perfection. These things may increase his life satisfaction, but his perfection is unalterable.

Likewise, doing undesirable, unproductive things will, most assuredly, diminish his life satisfaction, but not his perfection.

What Does Being Perfect Get Me?

> "Okay, let's say I'm perfect," Glumbunny adds, "so what? You said I'd still have to work to improve myself, I'd still have problems, I'd still struggle to find happiness, what does my perfection get me?"

Knowing that we are perfect helps us in many ways. Here are some:

1) It boosts our feelings of self-love and self-esteem.

Understanding that we are perfect at being who we are,
means we occupy a unique position that no one can
ever take from us. This alone will raise our feelings of
caring and worthiness about ourselves.

2) It helps us deal with failures.

Since failure won't diminish our perfection, we start to
see each failure as just a bump-in-the-road, not a
catastrophe.

3) It helps us deal with rejection from others.

Accepting our perfection lets us see that if others
reject us, it just means they are looking for qualities we
don't happen to possess. That speaks volumes about
them but does not diminish who we are.

4) It helps us be more honest in our dealing with others.

When we accept our perfection, it makes it easier for
us to be honest about who we are with others. Why
would we want to hide the best, our most authentic
self, from anyone?

5) It's wonderful for helping us find close friends and loving
relationships.

Embracing our perfection shows us how foolish it is for
us to mask who we really are when seeking loving
relationships. It's best for each person to fully see the
other. Rejection does not make us less perfect. What
we want is to find someone who appreciates our
perfection as we do theirs.

6) We don't have to be so judgmental with ourselves.

Understanding our perfection helps us to better handle
whatever life brings. It also defuses our self-judgments
over our responses to life events.

Accepting our perfection is not egoistic, not dishonest, and does
not force us into becoming someone we are not; it is already who we
are. Perfection seen this way is freeing, genuine, and enhances our
journey to happiness.

PERFECTION EXERCISES

Exercise #1: Seeing Yourself As Perfect.

You need to see that your perfection is an effortless expression of who you are; an appreciation for your unique qualities. Just as no two snowflakes are identical, no two people are exactly the same. In this view, perfection is really a celebration of our differences. What a concept: celebrating our uniqueness!

Make a list of the ways in which you differ from others. It may be through certain unusual qualities or characteristics you possess or perhaps the way you manifest them. Be as honest and clear as you can. This list is to show you the richness of who you are. Include everything, even those things usually thought of as negative.

Here is how Glumbunny began his list:

My Personal Qualities (positive or negative):
1) I'm very responsible. If I say I'll do something I do it.
2) I am caring but don't show much emotion. I often come across as cold or aloof, but inside I feel very deeply about my family, friends, and things I care about.
3) I'm judgmental, but working on becoming less so. I really believe people should not break the law, be cruel, lie, cheat, and so on. And those who do make me mad.
–Etc.-

My Abilities (or inabilities):
1) I am gifted at math and enjoy solving difficult numerical problems.
2) I'm not a people-person. I find it hard to figure out what other people mean unless they come right out and say it.
3) I'm a voracious reader and often learn more from reading about a subject than from hands-on training. I learned how to play a decent game of golf just by reading a book.
-Etc.

Other possible category headings include: Physical Qualities, Inner Qualities, Fears, Likes, Dislikes, Feelings About Animals, etc.

You can use any category you'd like in order to reflect your unique attributes.

Remember to include the so-called negative qualities. Within your perfection there is room for those as well. If there are things about yourself you wish to change, consider doing so; changing won't detract from your perfection.

<u>**Exercise #2**</u>: Seeing Others As Perfect.

Now do Exercise #1 with other people, your spouse, children, friends, coworkers.

If you enjoy biographies of famous people, do this exercise for some of them. Notice that even the greatest people who have ever lived possessed, as part of their make-up, qualities usually considered to be negative or imperfect.

❈ ❈ ❈ ❈ ❈ ❈

"We seem to be running out of happiness keys."

"Yes, Glumbunny, just one more, but it's a good one. None are more important to happiness than this last one."

"Good! I was hoping to finish on a high-note."

"Absolutely! Move right to Chapter 14, 'Present-Moment Living;' I know you won't be disappointed."

14

It's Now Or Never

Happiness Key #12: Present-Moment Living

> "The only way to live is to accept each minute as an unrepeatable miracle, which is exactly what it is: a miracle and unrepeatable."
>
> – Storm Jameson

Real living can happen only in the present moment, yet most of us spend but a tiny fraction of our lives there.

"Hold on," Glumbunny interrupts, "I've heard about how I should live more in the present moment. Maybe it's just me, but where else can I be but in the present? Here I am, right here, right now, in the present moment. What's the big deal?"

Like Glumbunny, many people don't get what all this fuss over living in the present is about. Let's take a look at how most of us avoid present-moment living and how we can live more in the now.

The Past Is Gone, Get Over It

> "Here lies my past, goodbye I have kissed it; thank you kids, I wouldn't have missed it."
>
> – Ogden Nash

Our thinking minds love mucking around in past thoughts and memories, imagining how much better things might have turned out if only we had said this or done that. Or sometimes we ruminate over how much better things were back then. "If only things could be that way now," we think with a sigh and a tear.

Many of us spend nearly half of our lives focused on the past. But the past has already happened. It's over. It's gone. Yet its hypnotic, siren-song continues drawing us to it.

Focusing on the past harms us because:

* We may develop guilt over something that went wrong.
  Guilt is a useless emotion that causes us pain without benefit. We cannot go back and undo anything that's happened; it's gone, it's over. What's needed now is responsibility, not guilt.

* We may become mired in romantic illusion.
  Dwelling on the past encourages us to romanticize it. Everything changes, that's the nature of life. When we stop insisting that things remain the same, we discover that the wonder and joy of the present moment always surpasses fixation on past, no matter how good it was

back then. The past is history, only the present is fully alive.

Let's Hear It For the Past

"Those who cannot remember the past are condemned to repeat it."

– George Santayana

Who among us has not spent delicious moments musing over past delights, victories, and loves? Happiness key number 9, "Handling Mistakes," showed us how important it is to review our past mistakes so we can learn from them.

It's not necessary to discard the past. The past, used wisely, can be fun and useful.

Spending <u>some</u> time in the past helps us:

✳ Learn the lessons of life.
>Our mistakes and victories carry lessons for us. Reviewing past events can teach us how to live more happily and effectively right now.

✳ Add the pleasures of sentiment and nostalgia to our lives.
>Remembering significant past events can be harmless and enjoyable. Still, it's important not to slide into romantic illusion. We become mired in romantic illusion when we compare the present unfavorably with the past and wish things could be as they once were.

>"Hmm," Glumbunny interjects, "I'll admit I'm very caught-up in the past. Sometimes I feel really guilty about things I've done or didn't do. Other times I find myself wishing things were the way they used to be. I spend a lot of time thinking about things like that. I'm beginning to see that I may be cheating myself."

Most of us spend far too much of our lives either roiling in guilt or immersed in escapist romantic illusion. Being trapped in the past keeps us from being fully alive in the present.

The Future: What Will Be, Will Be

"Cease to inquire what the future has in store, and take as a gift whatever the day brings forth."

– Horace

When not reliving the past, many of us spend much of the rest of our time focused on the future. We oscillate between guilt over what's already long-gone and worry about what the future will bring. The future is no more real than the past. The future hasn't happened yet. Many studies show that most of the things we worry about never happen. Still, this doesn't stop our worry.

Like guilt, worry is a useless emotion. By draining energy and paralyzing our ability to think clearly, worry robs us of any hope for taking effective action. The alternative to worry is planning. Planning helps us prepare effectively for future events.

Focusing on the future is harmful because:

✳ It leads to worry.
> Worry is a useless emotion. Worry exaggerates worst case scenarios, it inhibits effective problem solving, and it directs our energy into ineffective panic.

✳ It leads to wishful thinking.
> Those who indulge in wishful thinking live in fantasy land. "Oh I wish I were smarter, taller, richer, etc., etc…" It's a way of escaping the present into some pie-in-the-sky future. While a bit of wishful thinking is harmless, it can become addicting and keep us from the present moment.

Many of us spend so much of our time and energy in the past and future that we have little left for the present. Still, just as with the past, there are occasions when spending time in the future may be enjoyable and useful.

Have a Nice Tomorrow

"Everyone has it within his power to say, this I am today, and that I shall be tomorrow."

– Louis L'Amour

So if wishful thinking and worry are the future's blind alleys, how can we spend worthwhile time there?

Spending time in the future helps us:

❋ Set goals which gives direction to our lives.
> Goal-setting helps us find our purpose. Basil S. Walsh said: "If you don't know where you are going, how can you expect to get there?"

❋ Plan action for expected future events.
> When I have a presentation to give, planning helps me successfully complete everything that needs to be done within the allotted time.

❋ Enjoy creating fantasies about the future.
> Fantasizing about the future, so long as we clearly understand that we are creating fiction, can be a harmless pleasure. But because it's easy to slip from innocent fantasy into detrimental worry or wishful thinking, fantasy should be used cautiously.

There are benefits and pleasures for us when we revisit the past or entertain the future, but these pale in comparison to what the present moment offers. Also, the two great useless emotions, guilt and worry, that hound the past and future, don't exist in the present.

The Precious Present

"The passing moment is all we can be sure of; it is only common sense to extract its utmost value from it."

– W. Somerset Maugham

We are truly alive only in the present moment. The half-second before this moment is already gone and the half-second after has not yet arrived. Nowhere can we experience life fully, in all its dimensions, but in the precious present.

Placing our consciousness anywhere but the present robs us of aliveness. It's like running on two cylinders instead of eight. Everything is less vibrant, less exciting, less satisfying.

Yes, we can learn from the past. Yes, we can find direction from the future. But, full experiential living requires, **demands** that we focus on the present.

> "That sounds really good" Glumbunny says, "but how do I do it? As I said earlier, here I am, right here, right now, in the present. Maybe it's me, but I don't understand how I <u>cannot</u> be in the present."
>
> "You're physically here but where's your mind, Glumbunny, your thoughts, your consciousness?"
>
> "Right here with me, aren't they? I'm confused. I think I need an example."
>
> "Of course, Glumbunny, that's a good idea. Also, you'll find more help in the exercise section at the end of this chapter."

Glumbunny makes a good point. Talking about living-in-the-now sounds rather like fuzzy, New Age psychobabble. Eyes glaze, yawns begin, even as heads nod in lackadaisical agreement. Real examples of present-moment living are always best.

In these examples, we'll look first at the surface and then deeper, at what goes on in the mind of someone who lives primarily in the past and the future as compared to someone living in the present. In these examples, Glumbunny illustrates the past/future approach, and Bob, the present.

Examples of Past/Future Vs. Present

A) The deadly cocktail party:

<u>The Surface</u>
Glumbunny and Bob attend a business cocktail party at a large, downtown hotel. Neither knows anyone else there. They each get a drink, and circulate. They agree to leave after an hour and a half.

<u>Beneath the Surface: Glumbunny (Past/Future Approach)</u>

"Well, the food looks okay but they don't have my favorite Scotch, too bad. I don't recognize anyone. I'd leave if I hadn't agreed to stay 'till nine.

"Damn, I wish I'd stayed home to watch Monday-night football. It should be a great game. Why did I come anyway? I hate cocktail parties. I never meet anyone interesting. What am I doing here?"

Beneath the Surface, Bob (Present Moment)
"I'll get one martini and nurse it. The food looks good, even some vegetarian stuff I can eat. Looks like lots of people came alone. Great! I bet I'll find someone who'll want to talk about something fun. Oh, there's someone over there, right next to the bamboo plant, I'll try him first."

Bob focuses entirely on each person he meets, and on what is being said. His conversations are spontaneous and without any predetermined destination. Each conversation takes its own unique twists.

❀ ❀ ❀

On the ride home, Glumbunny complains, "I had a terrible time. The food was so-so and the Scotch barely passable. I talked with only two people and they were just as bored as me."

Bob loved having stimulating conversations with people he'd never met.

Glumbunny didn't let himself experience the present moment. He had a bad time because he focused on wishing he were somewhere else.

Bob's first decision was whether or not he would stay at the party. Deciding to stay, he made sure he got everything out of what that time and place held for him. He didn't second-guess himself, but plunged right in.

B) The lousy movie:

The Surface
Glumbunny and Bob go to a highly acclaimed Independent film.

As the lights dim and the movie starts, both realize it's a period-piece, a genre neither favors. Nevertheless, after ten minutes, Bob decides to stay; Glumbunny never even considered that he had the option of leaving.

<u>Beneath the Surface: Glumbunny (Past/Future Approach)</u>
"Oh geez, I should have checked, I hate period-pieces. And subtitles! I hate subtitles! So many good movies and we had to pick this loser. I'm gonna hate this. I've never seen any of these that are any good. I don't see why the critics love 'em so much. Well, maybe I'll just snooze through it. Oh, I can't, I'd be embarrassed if I started snoring. "

<u>Beneath the Surface: Bob (Present Moment)</u>
"Uh-oh, I didn't realize this was a period-piece. Well, let's give it a chance."
❈ ❈ ❈
"Hmm, doesn't seem too bad, I guess I'll stay."
❈ ❈ ❈
"Gosh, the dialog seems stiff, the characters wooden, and the plot really drags, but the costumes are great! And the visuals are so real that it feels like I've been transported back to the 17th century."
❈ ❈ ❈
Later, over coffee, they discuss the movie's failings. Bob loved the visuals, but tones down his enthusiasm so as not to upset Glumbunny who can't stop ranting about what a terrible movie it was.

Glumbunny, based on past experience, decided he was going to hate the movie. It never occurred to him to consider leaving. He also didn't try to find something to like about the movie. Wishing he were somewhere else, he glazed into resentful semi-consciousness.

Bob, seeing that it was a period-piece, not his favorite, considered leaving. But after deciding to stay, he found something about it to enjoy: the costuming and scenery. He had a good experience even though he recognized the movie's shortcomings.

C) The disappointing Restaurant:

<u>The Surface</u>
A new Chinese place just opened nearby. Glumbunny and Bob decide to give it a try. They both

love Chinese food and are always on the look-out for good, reasonably-priced, neighborhood restaurants.

They are seated promptly at a well-located table in a busy room. A friendly waiter greets them, makes suggestions, answers questions, and takes their orders.

The food arrives, but everything is bland, overcooked and flavorless.

Below the Surface: Glumbunny (Past/future Approach)

(On entering) "Hmm, clean but too plain. This place needs more zip."

"Oh dang! It's Cantonese! Why couldn't it have been Szechuan or Mandarin? I should have checked first."

❈ ❈ ❈

(The food is served) "Oh, no! Limp, overcooked broccoli drowning in brown, salty sauce. We should have gone to the Italian place across the street; I know they're good. What a waste of time and money! Next time I'm gonna let someone else try these new places first."

Below the Surface: Bob (Present Moment):

(On entering) "They're not much on decor, but it's clean and comfortable. Hmm, Cantonese, I usually prefer Mandarin. Well, let's have an adventure and give it a try.

"This waiter really knows the menu and is very helpful. If the food's as good as he is, we're in for a treat."

❈ ❈ ❈

(The food is served) "Mmm smells great. And he even remembered to bring the extra Chinese mustard and chopsticks; he's an excellent waiter."

❈ ❈ ❈

"Uh-oh, this stuff's really bland and overcooked. They're going to have to improve if they're going to make it, even with a great waiter. He's amazing. He obviously loves his job. It's fun watching him take care of all these tables and have so much fun doing it. He's a true artist."

❈ ❈ ❈

On the way home Bob acknowledges that the food wasn't very good. But still, he tried a type of food he rarely eats and witnessed a great waiter work the room.

Glumbunny just grumbles about how he wasted so much time and money on boring food. He hadn't even noticed the waiter.

Bob didn't have to pretend he liked inferior food in order to have a pleasant restaurant experience. Once he decided to stay, he found something he could enjoy, an outstanding waiter. While still maintaining his critical faculties, he didn't let anything ruin his experience of the moment.

Glumbunny discovered what he <u>didn't</u> like and clamped onto it with bulldog tenacity. He then dove headfirst into the past and future, berating himself for what he hadn't done and wishing he were somewhere else.

Maximizing Present-Moment Living

Here's how to get the most from present-moment experiences.

* First Step: consciously decide whether or not to participate. Many activities don't **require** our presence. We can choose whether or not to participate. If we decide to stay, we owe it to ourselves to find something there to like.

* Second Step: open up to everything this experience has to offer, sample it all.

* Third Step: from this sampling, select what we like most and focus all our of present-moment awareness on it.

* Fourth Step (optional critique): concentrating on what we like won't destroy our critical faculties. We won't become shallow, indiscriminate blockheads. Still, critique is best saved for later so it won't keep us from enjoying our present moment experience.

Don't Cheat Yourself

*"I have the happiness of the passing
moment, and what more can mortal ask?"*

– George R. Gissing

It is only in the present moment where we can be fully alive. The late artist Al Hirschfeld knew how to take advantage of present-moment experiences. In a Time magazine interview he was asked, "Do you ever get tired of the theater?" His answer: "No, there's always something that works, no matter how bad the play is. It will be the set, or one acting performance is outstanding, or the ushers [laughs] ... "

Yes, there is value to the past and future. Reviewing past events helps us learn valuable lessons. Acknowledging the future helps us with planning and goal setting. But we experience real living only when we are in the precious present.

PRESENT-MOMENT LIVING EXERCISES

Exercise: Select an Activity.
Choose something you'll be doing soon. Something like:
* Going to a play or a movie
* Going to a cocktail party
* Having dinner at a friend's house
* Going to the dentist (ugh! Maybe save this for the advanced course)
* Going to a museum
* Putting on a garage sale
* Going sailing
* Playing golf
* Really, anything at all

Before or shortly after you begin the activity, consciously decide whether or not to participate. If you choose to leave, leave (unless it's your dental visit; leaving will anger the dentist and won't be good for your teeth).

If you decide to stay, pay attention to what's going on, especially the things you like and enjoy, and then dive in to get everything you can from the moments you are there.

In the beginning, you'll probably find yourself zeroing in on what you don't like. That's okay. Stay conscious, and when this happens, notice it and let it go; don't dwell on it. Your mind is afraid you might miss some of the negative stuff that it loves to whine about. As you use this process more and more, your mind will become better trained to focus on the parts of the experience you like, and will trust that you can recollect those juicy bad parts later, if you decide to indulge in a postmortem.

This exercise is especially powerful when you use it for something you wish you didn't have to do, but can't get out of. Placing all your attention on the present will help you enjoy what would otherwise be deadly.

❄ ❄ ❄ ❄ ❄ ❄

"Hmm," Glumbunny utters, "so that's it, all 12 keys?"

"Yes. Did you have any trouble understanding any of them?"

"No, they're not hard to grasp. And as I've been doing the exercises, I'm actually beginning to feel happier. "

"Yes, Glumbunny, you're stoking-up your happiness factory."

"Yeah, but you know what? Some of my friends don't seem so pleased about my changes. What's that about? They're really good friends, too, some I've known since I was a kid. They've always wished me the best. Maybe I'm crazy, but it seems like they resent that I'm becoming happier."

"No, Glumbunny, you're not crazy. Even happiness creates problems. There are roadblocks along the path to happiness. You'll need to know about them in order to get past them. Part III: 'Detours Along the Happiness Highway' will help you deal with these roadblocks."

"Oh great! I thought becoming happier would solve my problems, not create more."

"No, Glumbunny, becoming happy won't get rid of your problems. But it will help you see the opportunities in your problems."

"Hmm, I hate to admit you're right, but I don't feel as frightened or overwhelmed as I would have before. I'm ready! Bring 'em on! I can absolutely do this!"

PART III: DETOURS ALONG THE HAPPINESS HIGHWAY

Note of caution to Glumbunny (and other readers)

If you've come this far and especially if you've done the exercises, it's likely that you're already happier than you were before. If that's the case, you may have observed what seems like resentment, or even anger over your progress coming from some of your friends, family, and coworkers.

It's ironic how often those who were the most supportive of your pursuit of happiness become resentful when you find it.

Still, this is not an unusual reaction. So, as you become happier, you should expect to encounter resistance from some of your friends, loved ones, and even society in general.

This section will alert you to the obstacles you may encounter as you travel along the Happiness Highway and will show you how to keep them from running you off the road.

15

The Happy Idiot

*"Men are the only animals that de-
vote themselves, day in and day out, to
making one another unhappy."*

– H.L. Mencken

Lynn is an executive with a biotech firm. Listen to what she has to
say about happiness. "I'm an intelligent, successful woman, but try as I
may, I've been unable to find lasting happiness. My friends and I talk
about this all the time, but none of us can figure out how to get it. We've
come to the conclusion that except for simpletons and nut-cases, it's
just not humanly possible. And I'm not willing to go through life as a
Pollyanna, laughing and smiling idiotically over everything, good, bad
or indifferent."

After years of fruitless search, many people reluctantly conclude that their hopes for finding ideal happiness are nothing more than childish fantasies. Holding to this belief, they surmise that anyone who seems to be too happy, especially without good reason, must either be a simpleton or is dreadfully out of touch with reality.

Let's now take a look at some of the negative tags pinned on the more happy by the less happy.

Sticks and Stones May Break My Bones, But Words Will Never Hurt Me

Happy people have been labeled as:

Village idiots:	"Anyone that happy can't be playing with a full deck."
Pollyannas:	"You're such a Pollyanna! You'd probably think it was fun to see your house burn down."
Out of touch with reality:	"How can you be happy while there are so many people in the world who are starving?"
Show-offs:	"He's not really that happy, he's just showing-off."
Delusional:	"I'm worried about Mickey; no one who's that happy could be seeing things right."
Being from another planet:	"I don't know what planet she's from, but it's not humanly possible to be that happy all the time."
Egotistical:	"Look at him laughing and smiling all the time. He thinks he's so much better than the rest of us."
Really annoying:	"Do you have any idea how annoying it is to be with someone who wakes up cheerful every morning?"

Is There Any Truth to These Charges?

"If a man is happy in America it is considered he is doing something wrong."

–Clarence Darrow

"Good grief!" Glumbunny moans, "Are you telling me that as I becoming happier, my friends and colleagues are going to think I'm either an idiot or a nutcase?"

"Hold on, Glumbunny, don't overreact. These criticisms are easy to overcome."

"Well, okay, but is there any truth to them?"

Let's look and see what's behind these accusations made against happiness.

<u>Village idiot</u>: Since few people enjoy ideal happiness, most conclude that those who do can't be normal. The truth is that except for those lucky few, like Smiley, who were born with a high happiness setpoint, developing ideal happiness requires intelligence, courage, and direction. This is the success formula for reaching all great goals, and ideal happiness is a great goal.

<u>Pollyanna, out of touch with reality, delusional, must be from another planet</u>: These are all variations of the same misconception: that long-term happiness is the byproduct of unrealistic optimism. Since no one knows what the future will bring, expecting a bad outcome is no more realistic than expecting a good one. Henry Ford once said: "Think you can, think you can't; either way, you'll be right."

Many people believe that having a pessimistic outlook will cushion them from the pain they get when bad things happen. It won't. Pessimism just adds worry, fear, and depression to the pain.

It comes down to how we wish to face the future: optimists welcome it while pessimists dread it. Optimism promotes happiness whereas pessimism fosters fear. Having an optimistic outlook doesn't mean we will ignore hazardous situations, nor will it keep us from taking appropriate action. Because expecting the best is unusual in our culture, optimistic people are often viewed with suspicion.

<u>Showing off, egotistical, really annoying</u>: Most of us wish we had more money. So, it's no surprise that watching some multimillionaire flaunting his wealth often breeds envy and resentment in others. Similarly, someone openly flaunting her happiness may anger others. Even

the National Football League recognizes this, and players who celebrate too much after they score touchdowns are penalized.

> "Great! Now I know **why** everyone I know will think I'm a happy idiot. But I don't want them think that about me! How can I stop them?"

Happy Idiot Solutions

Medical science knows that disease prevention is superior to treatment. The same is true here. Ideally, we'd like everyone to value and accept us, happiness and all. Our good friends and loved ones know that happiness hasn't turned us into idiots. However, more casual acquaintances may interpret our happiness as a symptom of happy-idiot disease. Using the toning-it-down technique described earlier is very effective for preventing this accusation.

Happiness Used to Hide Unhappiness

As our happiness increases, it's possible, even likely, that some will question whether or not we are really are as happy as we seem. This is because true long-lasting happiness is rare, while people using happiness as a shield to hide their unhappiness is common. This certainly was the case for Melissa.

> Melissa had it all. This 35-year-old traffic-stopping beauty was adored by her husband Frank, a physician, and Trudy, her bright, beautiful seven-year-old daughter.
>
> She worked part-time as an actress and model, appearing in national commercials as well as numerous ads in popular magazines.
>
> What's more, her sunny disposition and infectious laughter brightened the spirits of everyone around her. Everyone, that is, but Frank.
>
> Only Frank knew the real Melissa, a moody, insecure, disaster-in-waiting who would sometimes become so depressed that he had to physically restrain her from jumping off their third floor balcony.
>
> Melissa kept her depression hidden from public view by feigning bubbly-happiness. She was such a good actress that no one but Frank knew the truth.

ness so rare, most people just assume that anyone who seems to be too happy must just be trying to hide their unhappiness from others.

But, as Freud once said, sometimes a cigar really is just a cigar!

Fran was worried. She had been seeing Alan for almost four months and things couldn't be better. He was considerate, romantic, and good-natured, too good-natured. It was his positive attitude that had drawn her to him, but nobody's that good. Nothing seemed to upset him for very long. It wasn't that he ignored his problems. Quite the contrary, he took care of whatever needed attention effectively and cheerfully. But nothing ever seemed to get him down for very long. It just didn't seem right.

In desperation she blurted out: "This can't be normal, can it?"

Warren, her therapist, lightly touching his fingertips together the way he always did when he was about to say something he thought was really important, answered: "No, this is not normal behavior. Clearly, Alan doesn't feel safe with you. He's afraid of letting you see his weaknesses, his flaws. He believes you'll think less of him, maybe even reject him."

"But," Fran sobbed, "I tell him all my problems, I confide in him."

"Men often feel that they shouldn't have insecurities, they think it's unmanly. Quite often they're in denial and try to hide their fears and sadness behind a veil of happiness. You'll have to reassure him. Let him know that it's safe to be vulnerable with you."

❋ ❋ ❋

Over the ensuing weeks and months Fran pleaded with Alan to open up, to share his pain with her. She swore she wouldn't think less of him, that he could trust her.

But, try as he may, and he really did try, he could find no deep sadness to confess. Oh, he told her about problems he had at work, even once detailing an argument he had with his boss. Still, his happiness was so solid that even his biggest problems couldn't shake it.

Eventually, Fran and her therapist were forced to accept that Alan's happiness was real, not just a screen he used for masking sadness or protecting his masculinity.

What If They Don't Believe Your Happiness Is Real?

Just as Fran and Warren were finally forced to accept Alan's happiness as being authentic, the close friends and relatives of someone who is genuinely happy will eventually be won over. Arguing and insisting that we are happy doesn't work well. To others it sounds like we may be "protesting too much." Time works best here.

Once again, for casual acquaintances, our old friend, "toning-it-down," works wonders.

"How Can You Be Happy When There Is So Much Misery in the World?"

"...genuine compassion is based on the rationale that all human beings have an innate desire to be happy and overcome suffering, just like myself. And, just like myself, they have the natural right to fulfill this fundamental aspiration."

–His Holiness, the Dalai Lama

While misery and depression rob us of strength, deep inner happiness furnishes us with energy for tackling our problems. Nevertheless, anyone who flaunts their happiness in the face of another's tragedy is displaying a serious lack of compassion.

But compassion is characteristically seen in those who are deeply happy. Insensitivity to the suffering of others is a quality seen in those who are self-absorbed, not truly happy.

Will unhappiness help feed starving people? Will misery assist those women sold into sexual slavery? Can despondency help fight senseless human slaughter? Of course not! Still, many, whether from guilt or simply unclear thinking, act as though their misery will help alleviate the world's problems.

"It seems to me," Glumbunny interjects, "that unless we become discontent with the way things are, we'll never be motivated to try and make them better. If we're happy all the time, no matter what, nothing would get done, would it?"

"You're right, Glumbunny, anger and dissatisfaction can spur us into taking necessary action."

"Doesn't that contradict everything you've just said?"

"Not at all, but once again, you've raised a good point."

Happiness in the Face of Disaster

"Do not lose your inward peace for anything whatsoever, even if your whole world seems upset."

– Saint Francis de Sales

Does having ideal happiness block our anger at injustice? Will it lead us into blissful acceptance of human atrocities or earthly calamities? Of course not. If it were so, then the accusation that happiness disconnects us from reality would be true. But as happiness becomes more and more the core of who we are, we'll want to experience all of our emotions, even negative emotions, because we know our deep happiness will protect us from being overwhelmed by them. Knowing this means we can experience them without fear.

Still, loudly proclaiming how wonderful life is while viewing or discussing serious problems would be callous and insensitive, qualities foreign to those with ideal happiness.

You Can Chase It, Just Don't Catch It

"Suspicion of happiness is in our blood."

– E. V. Lucas

The Bill of Rights gives us the right to "… life, liberty and the pursuit of happiness." And while society supports our pursuit of happiness, it is suspicious of any who actually get it. This is at the heart of all "happy idiot" accusations.

It would be best if we could change this schizophrenic attitude. But so long as ideal happiness remains unusual, this attitude is likely to persist. People don't like it when someone else has what they, themselves, want, but don't have. So, until society's attitudes toward those who succeed in finding true happiness changes, some degree of toning-it-down will be needed by those who have found ideal happiness.

16

Fear and Loathing

"The strangest and most fantastic fact about negative emotions is that people actually worship them."

– P.D. Ouspensky

Fear, anger, guilt, rage, melancholy, shame, worry, anxiety, jealousy, and all the other so-called negative emotions bedevil us today just as they have throughout human history.

"But as my happiness increases, I won't have 'em anymore, right?"

"No, Glumbunny, you'll still have negative emotions."

153

> "But, I thought that as I got better and better at
> operating my happiness factory, they'd fade away."

Developing ideal happiness won't eliminate negative emotions, and that's a good thing. Who wouldn't want to feel anger when provoked, fear when attacked, outrage at cruelty, and sadness in the face of human suffering? In fact, <u>deep inner happiness allows us to more fully experience all emotions because we know they won't overwhelm us</u>.

The problem with negative emotions is not that we have them, but the degree to which so many of us allow them to dominate our lives. Many so-called normal people are either controlled by their negative emotions or live in constant fear of being engulfed by them.

Psychiatrist David Viscott considered those who respond to the events in their lives with a pattern of exaggerated negative emotions, especially when those emotions were driven by hidden feelings, to be neurotic. Neurotics live very painful lives.

> "Hold on. You're losing me here. Earlier, didn't you
> say we should experience all emotions, even the nega-
> tive ones?"
> "Yes, Glumbunny, that's what I said."
> "But now you're saying that anyone feeling them
> too much is neurotic, right?"
> "You heard right."
> "I'm confused. Can you clear this up for me,
> please?"

Everything in Moderation

> *"To everything there is a season,*
> *A time for every purpose under heaven ...*
> *A time to weep, and a time to laugh,*
> *A time to mourn and a time to dance."*
>
> – Eccl. 3:1, 4

In Chapter 14, 'It's Now or Never,' we saw that spending too much of our lives in the past and future keeps us from living in the present moment. But the past and future, as long as we don't dwell there too long, can be useful. The same is true for negative emotions.

Sometimes anger can propel us into taking necessary action, fear may warn us of hidden danger, grief may help us recover from loss. There is even a kind of bittersweet value to sadness.

> "So you're saying I should embrace anger, culti-
> vate worry, and court guilt?"
> "Glumbunny, no, no, and no. There is no need to
> pursue negative emotions."
> "But if they can help me, shouldn't I work on get-
> ting them right?"

Negative emotions are like jalapeno peppers: a little goes a long way. There's no need for any of us to cultivate our negative emotions. We all have more than we need. We can do everything possible to reduce or eliminate them without fear of getting rid of them entirely. Unchecked negative emotion can cause a multitude of mental and physical diseases, can destroy happiness, and even ruin our closest relationships.

Social Support for Negative Emotions and Neurosis

We all know the pain that accompanies negative emotions, and our heart go out to those engulfed by them. This social compassion is reflected in the plethora of governmental programs, support groups, and mental health projects, all intended to help those consumed by their negative emotions.

Also, many who are tormented by fear, worry, and the other negative emotions develop a cadre of friends and family to whom they can turn when they feel overwhelmed.

Certainly, anything that we can do to relieve their misery should be done. But, ironically, the help they get, more often than not, locks them more firmly into their self-destructive patterns.

> "Whoa! Hold on a minute. My wife's cousin, Janice,
> is a real worrywart. Last week she called at 2:00 A.M.
> in a panic over some cockamamie story she read in
> the paper about the end of the universe. She was terri-
> fied that the earth was about to wobble off its axis and
> we'd all die. It took my wife and me two hours to calm
> her down.
> "Are you telling me that instead of helping her,
> we're making things worse?"

Gradually, through a process of elimination, the neurotic's support circle is reduced to those few who are willing to spend hours listening to their fears, worries, and compulsions. Unfortunately, without professional help, these emotional eruptions will usually go on unabated.

Neurotics may be emotionally challenged, but they're not stupid. Deep down, they know their emotional patterns have dictated which of their friends have gone and which have stayed. They can see that breaking free of their neuroses could cost them their small support circle, and this makes it even harder for them to break free of their emotional chains.

Happiness and Life Events

> *"If you are distressed by anything external, the pain is not due to the thing itself but to your own estimate of it; and this you have the power to revoke at any moment."*

> – Marcus Aurelius

"New Study Finds Drug Use Increasing Among Teens." "Oil Cartel Raises Prices Again." "Terrorists Hold Two Americans Captive." "Drought in East Africa, Thousands Starving."

In Chapter 7, which discussed acceptance, we learned that inner happiness is not only possible despite painful circumstances, but is our best strategy for combating them.

Nevertheless, the commonly held view in our society is that external events **should** determine our mood. From this perspective, even minor irritants trump happiness.

> "Yeah, that's what I used to think," Glumbunny says. "But as my friends see that I don't let that happen to me anymore, maybe they'll want to change, too."
> "Some will, Glumbunny, but most will probably think something's gone terribly wrong with you."

Remaining happy when the TV repair person is two hours late, or when Sears fails to credit our account for a return, or when the computer doesn't do what we want, is considered abnormal. There is social support for allowing upsets, small and large, to pull us down, even for letting them ruin our entire day. Violating this social convention separates us from others.

"Wait! Let me solve this one."
"Sure, Glumbunny, what's the answer here?"
"Toning-it-down! Am I right?"
"You got it, Glumbunny, you're right."
Glumbunny, pumping his fist, shouts, "All right!"

Yes, here, once again, the simplest, best way for us to avoid separation from others is to use our old friend, toning-it-down.

Three Useless Emotions

While some negative emotions, in certain circumstances, can benefit us, there are three that cause nothing but misery and suffering. The three great useless emotions are, jealousy, worry, and guilt.

Jealousy

"O! beware, my lord, of jealousy;
It is the green-eyed monster which doth mock
The meat it feeds on..."

– Shakespeare, Othello

It's been said that all positive emotions spring from love and all negative ones from fear. Jealousy arises when we compare ourselves unfavorably to others. We're never rich enough, smart enough, tall enough, good enough, or sexy enough. Jealousy comes from feelings of inadequacy combined with fear of loss.

Is jealousy natural? Are we born with a jealousy potential quietly waiting for the right set of circumstances to emerge?

Certainly, something like jealousy is sprinkled throughout the animal kingdom. Fighting by dominant males over turf or mates, and rigorously enforced pecking orders, could be seen as a kind of natural jealousy.

"I'm glad to hear you say that jealousy is natural. I've been jealous all my life; I'm still jealous. I'm jealous when a colleague lands a big account or gets a promotion. I'm jealous of rich people. Heck, I'm even jealous when someone talks too long with my wife at a party."

"Glumbunny, you're not alone."

"I hate it! But you're right, it's useless. It gets me nothing but misery. But if it's natural, I guess I'll never get rid of it, will I?"

"Don't give up, Glumbunny, there are ways for minimizing it."

"Easy for you to say, Mr. Perfect, you've probably never been jealous in your life, have you?"

I know jealousy well because there was a time when it ruled me. I've never forgotten how powerless I felt in its grip. In fact, my own jealousy was the first negative emotion I worked on changing because it felt so awful. Here's my jealousy story.

My Shocking Jealousy Story

I was tired, but it was a good tired. We had finally taken the hard-fought doubles match, two sets to one, over our regular Sunday morning tennis opponents, Pam and Nate.

Judy and I lived in adjacent apartments in the same building as Nate and Pam. It was the spring of '72. Judy's marriage had ended six months earlier; I'd been single for two years. It would be another six months before we married.

After the match, the four of us trekked back to Judy's apartment for brunch where it was Pam's turn to be chef. Judy put Elton John on the stereo while I opened a bottle of champagne … and then another … and yet another.

At the opening bars of "Take Me to The Pilot of Your Soul," a more than slightly inebriated Nate jumped up, comically gyrating in sync with the music. He was quickly joined by an equally tipsy Judy.

Dark clouds quickly gathered. Throbbing music morphed into a clamor of hammers cracking my cranium. "Nah-na-**na**, nah-na-**na**, nah-na-na-nana-na-na-**na**!" Whirling dancers, a blur of dervish-synchronicity. "Take me … **take me** … **TAKE ME!** …" Skull swelling with each beat. "… to the wu-hun dangeh zone … " Eyes filled with blood. Heart sinking, watching … watching **enraged**. Watching … waiting. Finally, coiled dancers spinning out of control, tripping … , falling to the floor, he on her. And there they stayed, immobile … giggling idiotically, **demonically!**

The malevolent monsters feeding on my brain are in full command. **They** jerk me up! **They** whisk me to my fallen prey. **They** grind my puppet-teeth. **They** control the vertical. **They** control the horizontal. I, in powerless fascination, watch as **they** clench "my" fist driving it straight to the point of Nate's jaw. **Krrack!!** No escape left!

Silence screams. The green-eyed monsters evaporate, leaving me to face the mess. How can the music know to end at precisely the right moment? Nate, beefy ex-jock football player, blinks once and calmly queries: "What's wrong, Bob?"

Pam's gourmet breakfast wasted, Nate and Pam slowly exit stage left.

"Whoa! You actually punched him?"

"Yup, I did, Glumbunny."

"I never would have guessed that you ... "

"I know, I was in the clutches of jealousy. It had, in an instant, turned me into a raging, out-of-control monster."

"I can't believe it. You really hit him? You're not just making this up to make a point, are you?"

"I am using it to make a point, but it did happen."

"But jealousy is so overwhelming, I don't see how anyone can defeat it."

"Glumbunny, when we get to Section IV, How to Change, you'll learn techniques powerful enough to tame even jealousy."

Jealousy Is Useless

Jealousy is useless because:

* It gives our power over to rage. We lose control of our words and actions. Jealousy moves us further from who we really are than almost anything else.

* It turns us into the most unattractive, unappealing, least desirable beings we can be.

* It's self-defeating. It actually encourages the results it was raised to combat. Was I more or less appealing to Judy after she witnessed my jealous rage?

* Its gains are not worth having. If my jealousy had somehow frightened Judy into staying with me instead of running off with Nate, I would have gained a frightened, resentful, angry partner.

Worry

"Worry never climbed a hill, worry
never paid a bill,
Worry never dried a tear, worry
never calmed a fear,
Worry never darned a heel, worry
never cooked a meal,
It never led a horse to water, nor
ever did a thing it 'oughter.'"

– Anon.

The second great useless emotion, worry, is so universal that it, too, is probably natural.

Worry is fear that the future will bring us things we can't handle; fear that we'll be bushwhacked by named or unnamed problems, surprises, or disasters.

> "I admit it, I'm a worrier, been one all my life."
> "It's good to hear you say that, Glumbunny. The first step to curing a problem is admitting that you have one."
> "Hold on. I didn't say it was a problem. Sure, worrying makes me miserable sometimes, but I believe it protects me. Worry alerts me to potential dangers."

Worriers are a very dedicated group. Despite a multitude of excellent scientific studies, all showing that the vast majority of what we worry about never happens, worriers are convinced they are just being realistic, sensible.

In addition, worriers never seem to notice that their worrying doesn't help them deal with whatever it is they're worrying about. Worry is enervating and, at its worst, paralyzes us from taking needed action.

Worry transports us into the future, into fear of the future. It robs us of real living which can only happen when we inhabit the present moment. Not surprisingly, worry disappears when we move into the present.

A really good worrier never runs out of things to worry about. If what they've been worrying over doesn't happen, they believe their worry was somehow instrumental in causing the good outcome. And when what they've been worrying about does happen, they don't seem to notice that their worrying didn't help prevent it.

"Well, maybe you're right about **excessive** worrying, but I still don't believe that worrying is useless."

"Yes, Glumbunny, you, like most good worriers, are loath to give it up. Even if it doesn't work, it feels so right."

What's So Useless About Worry?

"Worry is as useless as a handle on a snowball."

– Mitzi Chandler

Worry is useless because:

* Studies show that up to 90 per cent of what we worry about never happens.

* Worry robs us of physical energy. This leaves us with little strength left to do something about what we're worrying about.

* Worry traps our thinking in a worry sinkhole. This blocks us from planning, the effective alternative to worry.

* Worry takes us out of the present moment, trapping us in the future.

* Habitual worrying harms our health because it leads to chronic stress and stress-related disorders.

The alternative to worry is planning. Predicting the future is iffy regardless of whether we're worriers or planners. Nevertheless, some future planning is necessary for us to live effectively in the world. Future things appropriate to anticipate include:

* Completing our income tax forms by April 15th.

* Finishing a work project by its due-date.

* Arranging for a future trip: airline tickets, travelers' checks, accommodations, itinerary, etc.

* Preparing for a lecture or business presentation: materials, slides, rehearsals, etc.

* Deciding when to start a family.

* Planning for when we die: insurance, a will, burial instructions, etc.

* Choosing the proper academic courses for a degree.

Unlike worry, planning is grounded in reality. Planning is the calm, effective, alternative to worry.

> "Yeah, my wife tells me I worry too much. She's always telling me I should stop. But that just makes me mad. Sometimes, I think I worry more just to spite her."
> "I know, Glumbunny, telling a worrier to stop worrying doesn't work."

My life partner is a great worrier. She could give the keynote at a worry convention: "Worrying Made Simple," or, "Worry No Matter What," or how about, "Sweat the Small Stuff."

I used to say to her: "What are you worrying about?", or, "Worrying won't solve anything," or "Don't worry, it'll be okay." All this good advice ever did was add arguing and resentment to her worry. Finally, it occurred to me that I was asking her to stop doing something she was really good at. Most people enjoy doing what they are good at. So now when she begins to worry, I say, without any trace of sarcasm, "Well, you are a great worrier, so enjoy it." This amuses us both and, at the same time, keeps us from conflict.

Guilt

"Guilt is the mafia of the mind."

– Bob Mandel

The last of the three useless emotions is guilt. Regret over our past actions or inactions creates guilt. Many parents use guilt to control their children. It's a powerful and effective weapon, but may lead to guilt-ridden adults.

We all felt guilty on occasion, so we know how miserable guilt can make us feel. Because it arises from things that happened in the past, the self-blame and regret we get from guilt just go on and on.

> "Just a minute, I agree that jealousy is useless, and maybe worry, too, but not guilt."
>
> "Why not, Glumbunny, what do you get from guilt?"
>
> "Well, for one thing, if I do something that harms someone else, my guilt shows them how sorry I am, that I didn't mean to hurt them."
>
> "I see, what else?"
>
> "Well, when I do something wrong, something hurtful or inconsiderate, I **should** have to pay for it. It's only right that I be punished."
>
> "Hmm, interesting; anything else?"
>
> "No, I guess that's about it."

Apologizing With Guilt

Even though guilt can't undo anything, many of us believe guilt shows we didn't mean it, that we intended no harm. Our guilt shows everyone what good, caring people we really are.

> "Yes, exactly!" Glumbunny throws in, "my guilt lets everyone know that I meant no harm."
>
> "But, Glumbunny, what about the injured party?"
>
> "Huh? What do you mean?"
>
> "You're using guilt to protect yourself, your image, but what about the one you harmed? What have you done to help her?"
>
> "Well, I would … , that is, I suppose I might … "

Guilt is the most perverse of the three useless emotions because it's entirely self-serving. Guilt places all of the attention on the guilty party: "Oh, **I'm** so sorry." "I would never have done that if **I'd** known this could happen." "Gosh! **I'm** such a terrible person." "**I'm** worthless" "**I** screw-up everything **I** touch."

In no time at all, a really effective guilty person will have everyone involved comforting **him**, reassuring **him**, hugging **him**, tending to **him**; while the injured party is all but ignored.

Guilt, the Avenger

Many view guilt as punishment for those who harm others, however unintended. We **should** feel guilty; we **deserve** to suffer. In this view, we've committed a crime punishable by flagellation with guilt. We get pain without gain. Everyone suffers and nothing improves.

> "That's just not true," Glumbunny interrupts, "guilt feels so bad that it probably keeps me from doing other hurtful things?"
>
> "Glumbunny, how many times do you mean to harm someone?"
>
> "That's a silly question, never! I would never *intentionally* harm anyone."
>
> "Right! When our actions, inactions, or words harm others, it's always by mistake, something we didn't mean. Those who actually intend to do harm rarely feel guilty about it. They're usually pleased by what they've done."

Responsibility Trumps Guilt Every Time

Chapter 11 showed us that we learn how the world works through our mistakes. Also, when a mistake occurs, responsibility is the best way for us to deal with the consequences. Responsible action always focuses on correcting or reducing the damage from our mistakes. Acting responsibly maximizes our learning and minimizes any harm our mistakes cause.

Guilt is so painful that it can inhibit us from initiating any actions where success cannot be guaranteed. Those who use this overly cautious approach to life reap only frustration, low self-esteem, and a life of quiet desperation.

Responsibility encourages us to learn from our experiences while protecting others from any harm coming from our inevitable mistakes. This, in contrast to guilt, helps us turn our lives into exciting works of art.

Finally, unlike guilt, responsibility focuses primarily on the victim rather than on the perpetrator's drama.

> "I think I get that" Glumbunny interjects, "but I could use an example because guilt is a tough one for me."

Example: Guilt vs. Responsibility

Borrowing a tool from a neighbor is a common occurrence, but one which may produce unanticipated problems. One such problem is that the borrowed tool may break. Let's look at two different ways for dealing with this problem, the guilty way and the responsible way.

The Event:

Ed wants to trim his overgrown hedges but it's not a job he fancies doing with his old hand shears. However, he knows that George, his next door neighbor, has a gas-powered hedge trimmer. George quickly agrees to lend Ed his power trimmer.

Everything goes well … at first. But then, while attempting to cut through a patch of particularly thick branches, the trimmer begins overheating. Soon, it sputters and dies. The acrid smell leads an alarmed Ed to reckon he's burned out the trimmer motor.

Ed's Guilty Approach

"George, I just ruined your trimmer! I'm so stupid! I should never have borrowed it; I never do anything right. Don't ever lend me anything again; you can't trust me. It's like I have this dark cloud following me everywhere I go."

"Ed," George tries to break in, "Don't be so upset, It's not that big … "

Ed interrupts, "When I was a kid my friends wouldn't let me play with their toys because I'd always break 'em."

"Really, Ed," George tries again, "I'll just take it over to that repair shop on …"

"I'm starting to feel a little nauseous," Ed moans, "I need to sit down. I hate this! Why me, God?"

George, concerned, says: "Ed, take it easy, don't make yourself sick. Come inside and sit down for a few minutes. You're overreacting. I'll get it repaired tomorrow; it'll be good as new. It needed maintenance anyway. It wasn't your fault. I should have lubricated it before lending to you."

"Why me, God?" Ed laments as he staggers against the door, "Why can't I ever do anything right?"

Ed's Responsible Approach

"George, I am so sorry," Ed says, "I think I may have burned out your trimmer motor."

"Uh-oh," George replies, "I should have oiled it before lending it to you."

"Well," Ed continues, "it was fine for a while, but then started overheating. Listen. I'll run it right over to Acme Appliance Repair on Main Street. They'll probably be able to fix it while I wait."

"Right now? Are you sure that's not too much trouble, Ed?"

"No, no," Ed goes on, "I broke it, so I'll fix it. I'll pay"

"Listen, Ed, let's share the cost. It's partly my fault."

"Are you sure, George?"

"Absolutely," George adds, laughing, "I'm just glad you're willing to do the leg-work to get it fixed."

Notice that Ed's guilty way diverts attention from the injured party and places it directly on the guilty one's drama, while his responsible approach focuses instead on helping the one who was harmed and in correcting the problem.

Experience All Emotions, Just Don't Go Overboard

"Moderation is best, and to avoid all extremes"

– Plutarch

We would be cheating ourselves if we didn't sample all of our emotions, even the negative ones. Still, we needn't try to augment negative emotions. They come aplenty without encouragement; it's the positive ones that need enhancing.

"Hold on, not so fast." Glumbunny interrupts, "What about the three useless emotions? If they're useless, why would we want to have them at all?"

"Very good, Glumbunny, there are two reasons. First, because tasting them helps us understand those who are tormented by jealousy, fear, and worry. Without first-hand experience, we wouldn't understand what they were going through."

"Oh, sure, that makes sense. What else?"

"Also, just because someone tells you negative emotions are worthless doesn't make it so; you need to form your own conclusions."

"Okay, got it."

Minimizing our negative emotions and maximizing our positive ones is a good formula for successful living.

Accentuate the Positive, Eliminate the Negative

"Positive attitudes – optimism, high self-esteem, and outgoing nature, joyousness, and the ability to cope with stress – may be the most important bases for continued good health."

– Helen Hayes

Positive emotions don't just make us feel better mentally, they are great for enhancing our physical well-being as well. Medical science now has proof that positive emotions really do make us healthier. Research show that laughter, humor, optimism and even prayer helps to boost our immune systems, reduce stress, fight cancer, ward off cardiovascular diseases, and even hasten our recovery from major surgery.

We also know that too much negative emotion leads to stress-related disorders.

"Okay, okay, I get it. Positive emotions feel good and are good for me. Negative emotions feel bad and are bad for me."

"Yes, Glumbunny, well said."

"So I should try to maximize all the positive ones and minimize the negative ones, especially the useless ones, jealousy, worry, and guilt."

"Excellent."

"So how do I go about doing that?"

Emotion Control

Happiness is much more than just another emotion; happiness is a way of being that fosters our positive emotions while inhibiting the negative ones.

Still, releasing negative emotions can be very difficult. We've learned that both society and our friends, despite good intentions, may lock us into them. Still, if we are to be truly happy, we must break out of the prison created by our negative emotions.

Section 4 offers some very powerful ways for changing negative behaviors and emotions. Many readers will be able to reduce their negative emotions and behaviors by using these techniques; I certainly have. However, for those who can't, professional help may be needed to help them escape their emotional traps.

❊ ❊ ❊ ❊ ❊ ❊

"Well, I guess we've covered all the roadblocks to happiness, haven't we?"

"Almost all of them, Glumbunny."

"Almost? There are still more?"

"We have only one more bump in the road to surmount."

"One more, huh, is it a big one?"

"It might be for some, Glumbunny, but I'm sure you won't have any trouble getting past it."

"Great! I'm ready."

"Okay, then let's go on to Chapter 17, 'Unhappy Genius.'"

17

Unhappy Genius

"[A] rose is a rose is a rose."

– Gertrude Stein

We learned in Chapter 12 that there is almost nothing in life that is either <u>all</u> good or <u>all</u> bad. So far, I've portrayed ideal happiness as being <u>all</u> good. It's time now to examine its blemishes.

Most roadblocks and objections to happiness are easily overcome or they evaporate under the gaze of careful scrutiny. However, several do have merit.

> "I can't believe what I'm hearing." Glumbunny gasps, "I guess I've just been assuming that ideal happiness really is all good. But you're saying that it's not?"

"Right, Glumbunny, even ideal happiness has some down sides."

"Incredible! I can't wait to hear what you have to say."

Happy People Like Everything

"When fate hands you a lemon, make lemonade."

– Dale Carnegie

As our happiness increases, our friends and acquaintances may start saying things like: "Oh! Don't ask Bob his opinion of the play. He likes everything." Or maybe: "Hank is such a jerk, but I bet you don't think so because you like everybody." Or perhaps: "It's been raining for two weeks, but you probably think that's great."

What such comments imply is that as we become happy we lose our ability to discriminate. That somehow, being happy carries with it the obligation to like everything and everyone, no matter what or who.

Frankly, this accusation is not easily dismissed. Once we've adopted Pollyanna's game and turned it into a habit, we will, in fact, find something to like about almost everything in our lives.

"But even so, happiness won't take away my critical powers, right? That's what you said."

"That's true," Glumbunny, "but most people won't see that. They'll focus instead on the 'liking everything' part and conclude that we have indeed lost our critical capabilities."

"So," Glumbunny asks, "what can I do to counter that?"

We could take the position that finding something to like about everything is simply a choice we've made, so why hide it? At first, some people may not take us seriously, but once they learn that this is just part of our being happy, most will drop their judgments and evaluate us based upon the totality of whom we are. Certainly, good friends and family, those who are closest to us, will recognize that our critical faculties are still intact. For others, using a little <u>toning-it-down</u> will help preserve our credibility.

Inverse Pollyanna's Game to the Defense

Grant, a happy friend of mine, taught me another approach that works wonders for countering the charge that happiness robs us of our critical capabilities. What he does, every now and then, especially with his most analytical friends, is to use Pollyanna's Game for finding something <u>not</u> to like, that is, an **inverse** Pollyanna's Game. I've tried it and it does help me retain credibility with others.

> "You lost me there, boss," Glumbunny interrupts, "how 'bout an example?"
> "Good idea, Glumbunny, examples always help make things clearer."

Here's how I use inverse Pollyanna's Game to find something **not to like**.

<u>Event</u>: My favorite football team wins the Super Bowl.
Playing inverse Pollyanna's Game, I might say:

* "Next year we'll have a tougher schedule."
* "Next year we'll be the number one target for all the other teams."
* "Now we have the poorest drafting position for adding new college players to the team."
* "Our players will demand more money now, and because of the salary cap, we won't be able to re-sign all of them."
* "I bet they'll raise ticket prices next year."

<u>Event</u>: I get a promotion at work.
Playing inverse Pollyanna's Game, I could say:

* "They'll expect much more of me now."
* "I'll have to travel and be away from my family more."
* "I'll have to work longer hours."
* "More responsibility means I'll have more stress."

<u>Event</u>: My daughter gets all A's in high school.
Playing inverse Pollyanna's Game, I could say:

* "Now she may become conceited."
* "Her friends will be jealous of her."

* "If she doesn't get all A's again next year, she'll be disappointed."
* "Now she'll want to go to an expensive elite university instead of the state college we can afford."

Notice, that there's nothing untrue about any of these negative assessments. Negative thinkers use inverse Pollyanna's Game all the time. The point is, an occasional negative comment will help maintain your credibility with others. Just don't overdo it. The last thing you want is to develop the habit of looking for the bad everything or everyone.

> "Glumbunny, you look dazed. Have I freaked you out?"
> "Yeah, I guess you could say that. This just seems to go against everything you've been teaching."
> "Yes, I understand. Using inverse Pollyanna's game should be used only for establishing credibility with others. Think of it as a variety of toning-it-down."

Once again, use inverse Pollyanna's Game only for bolstering your credibility with others. It works but has toxic potential, so use it with caution.

Happiness Breeds Complacency

> *"What distinguishes what's alive from what's dead is growth, be it in plants or in you."*
>
> – Wayne Dyer

If true happiness is Aristotle's goal of goals, wouldn't those who get it become self-satisfied, maybe even lord their happiness over others?

I've not seen self-satisfaction or complacency develop in anyone I know who has a high degree of ideal happiness. That's not to say it can't happen. Anyone on the path to ideal happiness is also being trained for a life of continued growth, the antithesis of complacency. Still, danger exists. Buddhism teaches us that every human virtue has what is called a near-enemy, a corruption that resembles the virtue but is distorted into a vice.

Glumbunny, looking confused, puts in: "I really need you to clear this up. You're starting to sound like my mother, lecturing me about good and evil and the temptations of the Devil. You can't mean that, can you?"

"No, Glumbunny, certainly not. I just want you to see how even happiness, if misused, might tolerate complacency"

"Well, does it?"

"Let's look at each of the Happiness Keys to see whether any of them are compatible with complacency."

We'll examine each happiness key to discover its relationship to complacency or self-satisfaction. I'll indicate a "Yes" for those that might support complacency, and a "No" for those that don't.

* **Key #1: Conscious Awareness**: Awareness, especially attention and inner awareness, connects us to our higher selves. So this key, which encourages continued inner growth, would certainly not support complacency.
  Score: No

* **Key #2: Self-Like/Love:** Those who truly like and love themselves would naturally extend that love to others. This leads to compassion and the wish to relieve human suffering. Still, self-love can be distorted into narcissism and self-satisfaction.
  Score: Yes

* **Key #3: Self-Esteem:** Because self-esteem is action oriented, those who have a high degree of it would be highly unlikely to become complacent.
  Score: No

* **Key #4: Appreciation/Gratitude:** Appreciation and gratitude require that we reach out and connect to both our inner and outer worlds. This active process is unlikely to foster self-satisfaction.
  Score: No

* **Key #5: Acceptance:** Using acceptance for everything could lull us into complacency.
  Score: Yes

✳ **Key #6: Responsible Adulthood:** Being responsible to ourselves and others promotes action and involvement and therefore is unlikely to foster complacency.
Score: No

✳ **Key #7: Non-Judgment:** Applying non-judgment might foster
non-involvement, thereby supporting self-satisfaction.
Score: Yes

✳ **Key #8: Pollyanna's Game:** Finding something to like about
everything is compatible with self-satisfaction and complacency.
Score: Yes

✳ **Key #9: Handling Mistakes:** Mistakes result when we take
new action in the laboratory of life, and this runs counter to
complacency.
Score: No

✳ **Key #10: Individuality:** Living in tune with who we are gives us
courage to act. But it might be stretched into giving us permission to become self-satisfied.
Score: Yes

✳ **Key #11: Perfection:** Accepting our own perfection in all ways
is congruous with complacency.
Score: Yes

✳ **Key #12: Present-Moment Living:** Living in the present says
nothing about self-satisfaction and is, in that sense, compatible
with it.
Score: Yes

So, the final tally shows five happiness keys which would not
support complacency and self-satisfaction, but seven which might.

> "Good grief!" Glumbunny murmurs, "Seven of the
> 12 keys actually encourage complacency. That's terri-
> ble!"
> "No, no, Glumbunny, none encourages us to be
> complacent."
> "Well, your own survey showed a majority do,
> seven to five."

"Glumbunny, you're taking this too far."

While some happiness keys help us to reach out and take positive action, others encourage us to let go of our limiting behaviors and beliefs. The five that promote action work against our becoming complacent. The other seven, the ones that help us let go, while not working against complacency, neither do they encourage it.

But, because it remains a possibility, however unlikely, complacency is an accusation against happiness we must take seriously.

Happiness May Damage Existing Relationships

> *"What's a joy to the one is a nightmare to the other."*

> – Bertolt Brecht

As we become happier, everything about us changes. While these changes are for the better, any change will affect those closest to us. After all, except for our birth families, our friends and lovers have chosen to be with us based upon who we were <u>before</u> we changed and became happy.

Change is something most of us resist out of fear. Our egos convince us that any change to the status quo represents potential danger and therefore must be resisted.

> "What you're saying is pretty scary. Some of my friends at work have started calling me, 'Mr. Happy.' Several have asked if I'm okay, or if something's wrong."
> "Yes, Glumbunny, they're beginning to notice that you're changing."
> "Even at home, my wife and daughters, who are thrilled that I'm becoming happier, are tiptoeing around not quite sure what to expect from me anymore."

Becoming happy is not just a personal event. It affects everybody around us, some more than others. We chose to make the personal changes necessary for us to have ideal happiness, while their inclusion in our action is imposed on them.

> "So," Glumbunny asks, "how can I help them ac-
> cept the new me? I do want to be responsible, after
> all."
>
> "Good for you, Glumbunny, you really are making
> progress."

It's important for us to alert close friends and relatives to our program for become happier so they won't be alarmed as they see us changing. Here, time is our ally. As our close friends see us becoming happier, most will be thrilled, but others may feel threatened by or even jealous of our developing happiness. Letting them know what's going on and reassuring them of our continued friendship is important. But, still, we may lose a friend or two.

Our birth families – parents, brothers, sisters, and cousins – will usually applaud our new happiness. But they still need to be warned about the changes we are making.

Our children are likely to be thrilled by our happiness. It's crucial to answer all their questions and reassure them of our continued love and commitment to them.

When one member in a primary relationship undergoes major changes and the other doesn't, problems can occur. It's always best when both partners cultivate ideal happiness together. When only one changes, the other may feel abandoned, left behind. In the worst case scenario, this can even lead to marital dissolution.

> "Oh dear," an alarmed Glumbunny moans, "I
> thought the tough part would be changing me. What
> have I gotten myself into?"
>
> "Glumbunny, don't be afraid. Your marriage is at
> little risk from your emerging happiness. Continue to
> reassure your wife and daughters that you love them
> and that your happiness will bring you even closer to-
> gether."
>
> "But you just said … "
>
> "Yes, but marital breakup is rare. It's unlikely to
> happen when those involved treat each other with sen-
> sitivity and love."
>
> "Well, thanks for the warning, I sure don't want to
> threaten my family. After all, I'm doing this to make
> things better for all of us."

Developing ideal happiness changes us and those closest to us. We must treat our friends and family with sensitivity to assure them of our continued love. In the long run, <u>our happiness will strengthen all of our closest relationships</u>.

Unhappy Genius

"Do not free a camel of the burden of his hump; you may be freeing him from being a camel."

– G. K. Chesterton

When we're happy, we access parts of our minds that are unavailable to us when we are not. Likewise, unhappiness and depression admit us to areas of our brains we can't reach when we're happy. I learned this, first hand, as I was going through each of my divorces.

During my first divorce, my tormented mind sought refuge in painting. Being unschooled, I was unable to make my paintings look anything like the subjects inspiring them, but they were powerfully expressionistic reflections of my angst at that time. I look at them today and marvel at their crude force and painful honesty.

A decade later, going through my second divorce, I wrote poetry. Once again, what I created was unsophisticated, but accurately mirrored the misery and sadness I was feeling.

I've never been able to artistically recapture the power and feeling of those times. I can't, because the despair that gave birth to that creativity is missing.

> "So, are you saying," Glumbunny intones, "that you wish you had more misery in your life so you could be more creative?"
>
> "Oh, no, Glumbunny, not at all. Those experiences, powerful though they were, hold no appeal for me now."
>
> "But, what about the painting and poetry you created, don't you miss that?"

Painting and poetry showed me that there is part of my mind I can reach only through misery. Powerful though it is, I have no wish to trade my happiness now for the pain of those times in order to paint and write like I did then.

But what if this were where my genius lay? What if my paintings rivaled those of the great masters? What if misery birthed poems that brought tears to all who read them? Might I not then choose inspired despondency over happiness?

Would Vincent Van Gogh have produced his incredible body of art without his lifelong agony? And if not, would he be better off being a happy but a mediocre artist? Would the world be a better place with a happy Van Gogh producing ordinary art, or a tormented artist producing masterpieces?

> "Whoa!" Glumbunny moans, "What a tough choice. Couldn't he be both happy and create great art?"
>
> "Possibly, but there is no guarantee. It would certainly be different."
>
> Shaking his head, Glumbunny murmurs, "What a choice, being miserable and great, versus being happy but ordinary."

Fortunately, few of us sit balanced on the horns of this dilemma. I suspect that those who do really have no choice; genius must have its way. And certainly there are others whose virtuosity can only be expressed through their happiness.

But genius must be served. And who would criticize those whose gifts require misery for choosing unhappy genius over happiness?

Give the Devil His Due

> *"Honest criticism is hard to take,*
> *particularly from a relative, a friend, an*
> *acquaintance, or a stranger."*
>
> – Franklin P. Jones

Honesty requires that we recognize that some of the criticisms aimed at happiness have merit. We've examined four of these: 1) Happiness may cause us to like everything and might dim our critical faculties; 2) Becoming happy may lead to us into complacency; 3) Developing happiness could damage our existing relationships; and 4) Developing happiness might separate us from our genius.

Critiquing this critique leads us to these conclusions: 1) Finding something to like about almost everything is by design and does not require that we lose our critical abilities; 2) Although happiness may theoretically support complacency, in practice, it rarely happens; 3) There is real danger that, if not handled well, our becoming happy could harm our closest relationships; and 4) In some cases, becoming happy could separate us from our genius.

"That's it, that's everything?" Glumbunny asks.

"Yes, those are the four objections to happiness that are worthy."

"Oh, good. My wife is thrilled that I'm becoming happier, so are my two girls. In fact, all three are ready to start working on increasing their own ideal happiness."

"That's wonderful, Glumbunny."

"Yeah, the relationship criticism is the only one I'm concerned with and I'm already preparing the rest of my family and close friends for the new me."

It's always best when our loved ones join us in developing ideal happiness. But if they don't, we need to prepare them for the changes they'll be seeing. Reassuring them of our unchanging love will help us keep our important relationships strong.

✳ ✳ ✳ ✳ ✳ ✳

"Glumbunny, you seem upset; what's bothering you?"

"Well, I'm doing fine with Pollyanna's Game. I've made it a habit and it's already helped me become happier."

"Good for you, Glumbunny."

"But now I'm trying to become less judgmental and I'm having trouble. I've done the exercises, but I'm still resisting."

"I'm not surprised. I know you've been judgmental most of your life."

"How can I change something so ingrained?"

"The next section, Part IV: How to Change, will help you make even major personal changes."

"Good, I need help."

"Okay, Glumbunny, this next section is just what you need."

PART IV: HOW TO CHANGE

"If you do what you've always done,
you'll get what you've always gotten."

– Anonymous

We come now to one of the most important sections in this book. Why? Because without change, everything else is nothing more than an intellectual exercise; a bit like **watching** a travelog to a wonderful destination instead of **being there** experiencing it.

Most people resist making changes, especially major personal changes. Yet change we must if we are to enjoy ideal happiness.

Chapter 18 will help us become the change-mavens we must be if we are to embrace ideal happiness.

18

How Can I Change My Life When I Can't Even Stop Biting My Fingernails?

"Change Your Mind, Change Your Life."

– Book title by Gerald G. Jampolsky
and Diane V. Cirincione

We Resist Change

It's ironic how much change, the one constant in life, is so universally feared and resisted. Forty, fat, and flabby, Frank embarks on an exercise program. A year later, his home has become an elephants' burial ground of abandoned fitness machines.

One entire room of Julia's four-room apartment is dedicated to piles of unsorted mail, must-someday-read books, store receipts going back eight years, and treasures purchased at garage sales. Finally, when she can stand it no longer, she takes a course on eliminating clutter. Despite early progress, six months later her mess claims a second room.

"Boy, can I relate to that!" Glumbunny exclaims. "I have this habit of chewing all the dead skin off my fingers, been doing it since I was a kid. A couple years ago my thumb became infected and it took weeks of antibiotics and bandages for it to heal.

"That scared me so I stopped. But after a month I was back chewing on 'em like gang-busters.

"Why is it so hard to change?"

Why *Is* It So Hard to Change?

"All changes, even the most longed for, have their melancholy, for what we leave behind us is a part of ourselves; we must die to one life before we can enter into another."

– Anatole France

Fear and habit work together to interfere with our attempts to change.

According to <u>A Course in Miracles</u>, all negative emotions spring from fear. Our ego, viewing change as a threat to its survival, fills us with enough fear and doubt to keep us from change, even when it's clear that change would make us better off.

Here are some ways the ego uses fear-thoughts to keep us from change.

* <u>Fear of loss</u>:
> Our ego tells us that changing will cause us to lose something or someone we value.

* <u>Fear for our security</u>:
> Our ego infers that change will endanger our safety and well-being.

* <u>Fear of failure</u>:

Our ego tells us that change is too difficult for us and that failing will damage our self-esteem.

✳ <u>Fear of disappointing others</u>:
Our ego insists that our attempts at change will fail, causing others to think less of us.

✳ <u>Fear that changing will take forever</u>:
Our ego rants that trying to change will commit us to prolonged suffering.

✳ <u>Fear that change will be bad for us</u>:
Our ego protests that change will just make things worse for us, not better; the devil we know is preferred to the devil we don't.

✳ <u>Fear of responsibility</u>:
Our ego tells us that change will make everything worse and we'll have no one to blame but ourselves.

✳ <u>Fear of success</u>:
Our ego insinuates that any success change brings will alienate our friends and family.

Habits, working in tandem with fear, help keep us from changing. Habits arise from recurring behavior. Most of our habits, being unplanned, rarely serve our best interests. The ones we've had longest are the hardest to break – things like smoking, drinking, overeating, and self-destructive thinking.

"You're painting a bleak picture," Glumbunny intones, "I'm getting discouraged. With opponents like fear and habit, how will I ever be able to make the changes I need for me to be happier?"

"Yes, Glumbunny, it's hard to change, but this chapter will show you how to overcome both fear and habit on your way to becoming a change-expert."

Imposed Change

"We change, whether we like it or not."

– Ralph Waldo Emerson

Despite resistance, we change anyway. Much of this is change we're required to make, change where we have no choice.

Mary's home is destroyed by fire, throwing her entire life into disarray. Sarah suffers a paralyzing stroke, changing everything in her life and forcing her husband, Jack, to change jobs in order to care for her. Frank is promoted to Vice President of his company, but now he and his large family must move to Dallas. A near-death experience leads Janice to question her view of what's important in life. She leaves her stress-filled, high-paying job to become a potter.

When required, most of us handle change, even major change, quite well. Nevertheless, our ego-minds strive to block <u>unforced changes</u> to preserve the safety-net of predictability it loves. Using fear and habit as primary weapons, our ego-minds work to keep us from all but forced change.

Change itself is not hard once we get our ego-minds out of the way.

Ways We Change

"The reality is that changes are coming ... They must come. You must share in bringing them."

– John Hersey

While undertaking voluntary change is hard for most of us, there are others who welcome change. I recall hearing psychologist and author Wayne Dyer say how much he enjoys change.

Let's look now at some of the factors that affect how well we take to change.

1) Hard vs. easy-changers:
   Some, like Wayne Dyer, embrace change as naturally as others resist it. In their view, change adds adventure to their lives. Still, easy-changers are as rare as snake toes.

2) Maturity/wisdom:
   Many of us who become wiser as we age find that changing becomes easier. On the other hand, aging without wisdom leads us to fossilized rigidity.

3) Trial and Error:

The more we learn from the laboratory of life through trial and error, the more we welcome change. Those who fail to learn life's lessons resist change more and more.

4) Hitting-the-wall:

This may be the most powerful change motivator of them all. It's also the most painful. Hitting-the-wall is when something catastrophic shakes the foundation of our lives. Examples include death of a loved one, bankruptcy, divorce, and major personal injury or disease.

Hitting-the-wall opens us to accepting major personal changes because the underpinnings of our lives have come undone.

But this opportunity comes with an expiration date. Once we've recovered from our misfortune, our old resistance to change comes right back.

5) Religious/Spiritual Awakening:

Those who undergo religious or spiritual rebirth may be so powerfully affected that they find making changes, even major ones, quite easy for them.

6) Coming to Decision/Intention:

Actually, it's not change that's difficult; what's hard is making the **firm, unencumbered decision** to change. This kind of decision I like to call **intention**. With intention, changing becomes easy. We'll be saying more about this one, shortly.

7) Change Techniques:

Many methods have been developed to help us succeed at change. However, even the most effective of these won't work for everyone. We'll be looking at change techniques a little later in this chapter.

Change Basics

"The world does not have to change ... The only thing that has to change is our attitude."

– Gerald Jampolsky

"Glumbunny, you're making a funny face, what's bothering you?"

"It's just ... ohh, I'm just not one of those 'easy-changers', I <u>hate</u> change! And now you expect me to become a 'change-expert?' I don't think so!"

"Many people feel as you do, Glumbunny, but mastering change isn't as hard as you think. Look, just keep reading because I know this next section will help you."

Wouldn't it be great if we could all change for the better any time we wanted? We'd stop smoking, eat healthier, exercise, lose weight **and keep it off**. Well, we can! But first we need to understand some change basics, and then, finally, learn some effective techniques for making change.

Here are some change basics:

1) The only person we can change is our self. Trying to change someone else almost never works.

2) It's always best to have a change-buddy; someone who supports us through the inevitable tough times. But, rest assured, even if this isn't possible, we can change all by ourselves.

3) Expecting change to be difficult can be a good mind-set because then setbacks will seem less discouraging. Remember, change requires that we overcome longstanding habits as well as our egos which view change as a threat. Just don't overdo it; anticipating severe difficulties can be inhibiting. It's not going to be **that** hard.

4) Don't delay starting. It may seem reasonable to wait for our schedules to become lighter. Recognize this for the ego delaying-tactic that it is. Life will always keep us busy. It's now or never!

5) Humor is a terrific ally. When it comes to change, Ann Richards, former governor of Texas, says: "Humor is a lifesaver for me." Stepping back and gently laughing at ourselves through the inevitable tough times will keep us on track.

6) There are many change techniques available. The best approach is to begin by sampling as many as possible but then stick with the one or two that work best.

How to Change

"Anybody can change completely and become anything he or she wants to become in moments."

– Wayne Dyer

"All right, already," Glumbunny interjects, "I get it! We're all afraid of change and I'll have to overcome my old habits. My wife said she'll be my change-buddy and I'll try to keep my sense of humor. But you said to begin now. I'm ready! When are you going to tell me how to do it?"

"Wow, Glumbunny, you are rarin' to go. Excellent! Right now is when you'll discover how to change."

While it's important to understand why we resist change and what factors influence it, change itself requires only two steps: 1) Coming to intention, and 2) trading old habits for new ones.

Step 1: Intention

Having intention is absolutely necessary for successful change. Because intention is so important, let's define and characterize it now:

> **Intention:** Having intention means: 1)we are clear about what our change-goal is, and 2) *there is nothing in our mind working against our change-goal.*

Intention is **the key** for achieving successful change. Both components of the above definition are important, but the second part is **vital**. When there is nothing in our mind working at cross-purpose to our change-goal, then **change becomes effortless**. This is important and should be clearly understood. Coming to intention is the hard part of changing. With true intention, change follows as naturally as night follows day. Without intention, change becomes a titanic struggle.

"Hold on," Glumbunny stammers, "so, for me to change all I have to do is just really intend it? I don't think so."

"Glumbunny, coming to intention is simple but not necessarily easy. Identifying and letting go of everything working at cross purposes to your change-goals can be challenging, to say the least."

"Perhaps an example would help clear this up for me."

"Sure, Glumbunny, how about something like losing weight and keeping it off?"

"That's a good one. I've lost weight more times than I care to remember, but it always comes right back."

As we know, many who are overweight can lose it, but keeping it off is another story. The problem is that they haven't made it their **intention**, at least not as I've defined it. Their diet is based on willpower. They deny themselves fattening foods but, deep down, still crave them.

Early on, when their self-control is strongest, they shed pounds, but eventually, as their resolve weakens, back they come.

The best way for losing weight <u>and keeping it off</u> is for us to eliminate <u>all</u> our "hold-backs." Hold-backs are those thoughts and beliefs we have that work at cross-purpose to our desired change. Removing these hold-backs is necessary for us to reach intention.

Some examples of cross-purpose thoughts are: "These pastries look delicious; it wouldn't hurt to have just one." "I've had a terrible day, I'll feel a lot better if I have barbeque for dinner." "I've been good all week; I deserve a big Mac and fries."

Once we've eliminated our hold-backs, we won't be tempted to cheat even when we see friends gorging themselves on our favorite foods. It may sound too good to be true, but <u>this is exactly how intention works</u>.

Step 2: <u>Trading old habits for new ones</u>

Psychologist Phil McGraw teaches that although we can't actually break old destructive habits, we can replace them, trade them for better ones. Once we've reached intention and successfully changed, we'll need to practice our new behavior long enough for it to replace our old, bad habit.

"Well, okay, I get what you're saying," Glumbunny interjects, "but I can't believe it's as easy as you're making it sound. Are you saying I should just tell myself I don't want the fattening foods I love? That sounds like the old willpower game to me."

"No, no, Glumbunny, willpower won't do it. What you need is a method for developing intention. With intention, you'll be able to make changes you never thought you could. You're about to learn some truly powerful techniques for making change."

Two Powerful Change Techniques

*"Once you become detached from
things, they don't own you any longer."*

– Wayne Dyer

There are almost as many methods for achieving change as there are those who want to change. The two described below are both potent and effective methods I've used to accomplish change.

Method 1: Twenty-two times eleven (22 x 11)

I first learned of this technique in Michael Domeyko Rowland's book: Absolute Happiness. I've used it successfully for losing and keeping off weight.

Here is how to use 22 x 11:

a) Write your goal in the form of a brief, declarative statement (see examples, below). Use positive, present tense terms. Write it as though the change you want has already happened.

b) Find a place and time when you will be able to work on this for a half hour on each of eleven consecutive days.

c) Write or type out your goal-statement 22 times, skipping one or two lines between each repetition.

d) Start at the top and read each goal-statement either aloud or silently. Record your reactions to each reading on the spaces you've saved. If you have no reaction, that's okay. Just write "nothing" or "blank" and go on to read the next one.

If an important insight arises, just note it and continue reading your 22 goal-statements. Return to it only after you've finished reading all 22.

e) This sequence must be followed precisely. Write the exact words of your goal-statement each time. Also, there must be no disruptions once you start and no days skipped. Turn your phone off so you won't be interrupted, and place reminders for yourself so you won't miss any days. If you are interrupted, you'll need to rewrite all 22 goal-statements. If any days are omitted, you'll need to repeat the entire eleven-day cycle.

f) If, after eleven days, you still haven't gotten the result you wanted, you may repeat 22 x 11, after waiting another eleven days.

g) When using 22 x 11, it's best to work on just one change at a time.

Examples: 22 x 11 Statements

Weight Loss:
    Poor: "I will lose twenty pounds in six months." (This statement is vague and not phrased in present tense terms.)
    Better: "I now weigh 160 firm, healthy pounds." (This statement is specific and in the present tense.)

Stop Smoking:
    Poor: "I no longer am a two pack-a-day smoker." (This is negative and not specific. Is she now a one or, perhaps, a three pack-a-day smoker?)
    Better: "I am now enjoying my smoke-free life." (This statement is clear and uses positive terms.)

Stop Judging Others:
    Poor: "I will stop judging others, knowing that this will help me become happier." (This statement is negative, future oriented, and unfocused.)
    Better: "I welcome and accept all the actions and ideas of others." (Positive, clear, and current.)

Of course, remember to apply the message of your 22 x 11 statement to your everyday life so it will become a habit. This change technique gives you a running start for replacing bad habits with good ones.

"It sounds too easy," Glumbunny offers, "do you really believe 22 x 11 can help me change?"

"Glumbunny, easy or hard isn't the issue. What's important is whether or not it works. First use it for small changes. Then, if you're successful, use it for your bigger ones."

"Okay," Glumbunny adds, "I've been wanting to drink less in the evening. I'm used to having two glasses of wine at night, but I fall asleep in front of the TV before nine o'clock. I'd like to have just one glass. How 'bout if I use it for that?"

"Sure, what would be your goal-statement?"

"Umm, let's see...how about: 'I am now fully satisfied drinking one glass of wine in the evening.'?"

"Well done, Glumbunny, go for it."

Method 2:   The What-Else Technique:

This powerful "What-Else" change-technique is great for uprooting entrenched negative habits and replacing them with new, better ones.

What-Else recognizes that we are getting something we want from our current behavior, even though we may not be aware of what we're getting. I call these hidden gains "hold-backs." It's hold-backs that keep us from developing the intention we need for successful change. Intention requires that we eliminate all the hold-backs binding us to our old behavior. What-Else helps us identify and then remove those hold-backs.

Here's how to use the What-Else technique:

a) Ask yourself what you are getting from your unwanted behavior, what gains. Unlike 22 x 11, your question may contain negatives.

Examples: "What am I getting by gaining back the weight I've lost?" "What am I getting by beating myself up over my mistakes?" The essence of the question is what's important, not its precise wording.

b) Find a time and a place where you will be alone and uninterrupted for about 30 minutes, preferably, someplace comfortable and dimly lit.

c) Sit down, close your eyes, and take several deep breaths to relax.

d) Either aloud or silently ask your question and listen for your answers.

Example: Question: "What am I getting by continuing to put on weight after I lose it?"

Answer: "I get to eat the fattening foods I like."

e) Now, ask yourself if you are willing to give up what you are getting from your unwanted behavior. For instance, in this case, ask: "Am I willing stop eating fatty foods?"

Consider carefully. This is a serious question. Don't say "yes" unless you truly mean it. If you can honestly answer "yes," then visualize yourself letting go of your desire to eat those foods and continue with the process.

If, however, you answer "No," then stop doing What-Else now. You won't be able to keep weight off, but at least you know why; it's no longer a mystery. This is a big step forward because you know you aren't a victim of some mysterious force. At another time you may be willing to give those foods up and try again.

f) After letting go of what you're getting, ask yourself once again: "What else am I getting from putting weight back on after I lose it?" Once again, listen for your answer. You may hear: "I can't afford a whole new wardrobe.", or "My friends might not like the new slimmed-down me." Or maybe even, "I'm afraid that losing weight might invite sexual interest and that really scares me."

g) As you dig deeper and deeper repeating your What-Else question, you may uncover a gain that feels like THE BIG ONE, the origin of your unwanted behavior. Giving that one up will feel like letting go of a burden you've been carrying for years. But don't stop yet. Continue asking yourself "what else?" until you get no further answers. This is your chance to clear out all the remaining hold-back strings.

Congratulations! You've just arrived at <u>intention</u>. The change you want will now happen <u>quickly</u> and with <u>amazing ease</u>.

h) You may reach intention after just one 30 minute What-Else sitting or may require four or five separate sessions.

"You know," Glumbunny pipes in, "this What-Else method makes sense to me. Still, I've never been successful at making major change in the past. Does it really work?"

"It's worked for me."

"But," Glumbunny persists, "will it work for the really big changes?"

"Well, I used it to defeat jealousy; you remember my jealousy story, don't you?"

"You bet, I'll never forget that one! If What-Else helped you eliminate jealousy then I'm really impressed. But it would help a lot if you would tell me exactly how you used What-Else to do it."

"Okay, Glumbunny, good suggestion."

What-Else In Action

It was a number of years after my jealousy story before I developed the What-Else technique. No, I didn't punch-out anyone else, but jealousy continued dogging my romantic relationships. And jealousy never helped any of them; it was all pain with no gain.

By 1984 I had already developed and used What-Else successfully for making small changes, so I was eager to try it for something big, like jealousy.

Using What-Else to Jettison Jealousy

Linda and I had been dating for about a year. While we enjoyed each others company, it was clear to both of us that our relationship was not "the one." By mutual agreement we were free to date others. Still, I often became jealous and sulky when Linda went out with other men. The time had come to give What-Else its toughest test: eliminating jealousy.

❋ ❋ ❋ ❋ ❋ ❋

It was a rainy, November evening in San Francisco. I unplugged the phone, lit a fire, and with glass of 1982 Mondovi Chardonnay in hand, sank into my over-stuffed recliner. The room, in twilight darkness, was silent but for the crackling of oak logs burning on the hearth.

I took six deep, slow, abdominal breaths to relax. What-Else kicked in as I watched the ravenous flames devouring the logs.

"What am I getting," I silently implored, "from being jealous about Linda seeing other guys?" I waited . . nothing … nothing. I asked again, this time aloud. Finally, a hesitant inner voice whined: "Well, your friends rally 'round comforting and supporting you when she sees other men."

"Hmm, yes," I acknowledged, "this is true. Well," I continued, "Are you willing to give that up?"

I played a mental video of me not wallowing in the jealousy-induced strokes my friends always gave me. "Sure," I realized, "I can give that up." Then, I felt myself letting it go. No problem.

"Okay, what else am I getting from my jealousy over Linda seeing other men?"

The dam, once breached, offered no further resistance.

"My dad was jealous of my mom. I idolized him, and when I'm jealous it makes me feel more like him."

"Yes, well, will you give that up?" As I considered, I realized there were certainly many better ways than jealousy for me to be like him. I answered myself: "Yes, I can give that one up too." As I visualized letting it go, <u>I felt noticeably lighter</u>.

"So, what else am I getting from my jealousy about Linda dating others?"

"When Linda sees that I'm jealous, she becomes very solicitous. She hugs me and tells me how much she cares for me.

"Can you give that one up?" The answer came back right away, "Yes!" And off it went.

❋ ❋ ❋ ❋ ❋ ❋

After 30 minutes I was exhausted, but felt much more in control. But, I knew I wasn't done. It took three more What-Else sessions before I discovered and released everything I got from being jealous.

The final hidden gain, the mother of all gains, emerged during the final session. It was the sense of control over Linda that I got from my jealousy. Discovering that I used jealousy for control was something I was delighted to give up. Releasing that one felt like releasing a fifty pound load I'd been lugging around for decades.

What-Else is powerful because it leads us to the origins of our unwanted behavior. Once we see what is keeping us captive, it's usually quite easy to give it up.

And, it works!

> "Well, I'm impressed," Glumbunny exudes, "I'm going to use What-Else as soon as I get home for getting rid of my number one problem, being judgmental."
>
> "Not a good idea, Glumbunny."
>
> "Wha…but…why not?"

No technique for change is likely to succeed unless, through actual experience, you have confidence that it will work. The best way to build this confidence is to use What-Else for making small changes first.

Using it to achieve small changes will build your confidence in the method; confidence you'll need for tackling your big changes.

Glumbunny has been having trouble getting up an hour early to meditate. He could use What-Else right away for achieving that. Also, he wants to begin taking a half-hour walk after work to improve his health. His wife has offered to go with him, but something always seems to get in the way. He could start by using What-Else to make this happen.

Other Change Tactics

Here's a brief description of some other change techniques:

Affirmations:
Like the statements in 22x11, affirmations are brief declarations stated positively, and in present tense terms as though the desired change has already happened. Write your affirmation on cards and post-its and placed them where you'll see them throughout the day.
Examples:
* "I now welcome all my mistakes for the valuable life-lessons they contain."
* "I am grateful for all that I receive everyday and for the gift of life on earth."

Writing out:
Writing out a goal on paper helps clarify and fix it in your mind. Doing this adds to the effective-

ness of practically any other change technique as well.

Learning by Example: If you want to lose weight, spend time with those who have successfully lost weight. If you want to eliminate jealousy, seek out those who aren't jealous. Being with those who reflect where you want to be will help you get there. The opposite is true too. Spending time with people who mirror your old, unwanted behavior moves you away from your change-goals.

Therapy: Mental health workers can help with desired change. I've been especially impressed with the effectiveness of cognitive therapy and psychocybernetics.

Happiness Coaching: Personal life coaching, a relatively new field, is designed specifically for those wishing to make positive life changes. I have recently adapted coaching techniques for helping people develop ideal happiness.

ENDINGS AND BEGINNINGS: WHAT NOW?

"Even if you're on the right track,
you'll get run over if you just sit there."

– Will Rogers

Beginnings and endings are another version of the old chicken and egg story. It's obvious that endings follow beginnings, but it's also true that beginnings come after endings. Our careers begin when schooling ends. Single life is over as marriage begins. Even the end of life could be seen as the beginning of the greatest adventure of them all.

Finishing this book means you are ready to begin your journey to ideal happiness. Take a look at the appendix where you'll find the

Happiness-Key Self-evaluation Form. Use it to score how well you believe you are doing right now with respect to each of the 12 happiness keys. The numerical scores you assign to each key are less important than how they compare to each other. Make several copies of the blank form for future use before completing it.

If you have difficulty making any of the evaluations, ask the opinion of a good friend, someone who's known you for many years. Your spouse or significant other may not be the best one to consult here; their evaluation is apt to be skewed by the dynamics of your relationship.

Date the completed chart and at intervals update your scores. This will allow you to plot your progress over time.

It's always best at the beginning to work first with those happiness keys where you're already strong. <u>Your progress will be faster and easier than if you start with your weaker ones</u>. This tactic will help you develop the confidence and momentum you'll need for tackling the tougher ones.

Start Now

In the world of "now and not-now," "now" means this very instant; a moment from now is "not-now." It is important to begin your journey as soon as possible. Delaying a few days is okay, but if you wait much longer, your resolve may erode. So begin as soon as possible. How you go about developing each happiness key is, of course, up to you. Here is one good way to begin.

Game-Plan

1) Make copies of the Happiness Key Evaluation chart in the appendix before completing it.

2) Score yourself for each of the 12 keys as suggested above and choose one of your strongest to work on first.

3) Obtain a notebook and title it: "My Happiness Workbook."

4) Reread the chapter concerning the happiness key you're starting on first.

5) Do, or redo, the exercises suggested for that key located at the end of the chapter.

6) Apply what you've learn to your daily life, keeping in mind that it will likely take at least three weeks before your new behavior becomes a habit.

7) At the end of each day, record all successes, failures, thoughts, or emotions related to your work and all your experiences with that happiness key. Note especially any surprises or insights you have.

8) Use 22x11, What-Else, or any other change technique you find that works best for you for making personal changes.

9) When you're satisfied with your progress, move on to your next happiness key. Once again, choose one with a high score until you've developed confidence in your ability to change, and in your change method.

10) Understand that progress is never smooth and steady; some backsliding is inevitable. Three steps forward and two steps back represents good progress.

11) Developing ideal happiness doesn't require that you achieve a perfect 100 for any of the happiness keys. Small improvements will stoke up your happiness factory, leading you to experience more and more happiness.

12) Increasing ideal happiness is a lifelong endeavor. But as your happiness increases, you will notice it becoming <u>easier</u> and easier to go higher and <u>higher</u>.

What If You Get Stuck?

If you get stuck or even if you just want to move faster, check out the books listed on the suggested reading list in the appendix. They are all excellent.

Personal happiness coaching is a very powerful way to progress. It is available by phone on a weekly, one-to-one basis. Go to my web-site, <u>www.happy4life.com</u> for more information. This web-site also lists my upcoming happiness lectures and training programs.

"Say," Glumbunny puts in, "I'd like to ask you something."

"Sure, fire away."

"May I join you and Layne for golf this Sunday?"

"But, Glumbunny, didn't you say you couldn't play on Sundays because of your mother's admonition to stay home and think about God?"

"Yes, that's true, I felt too guilty to do anything, even though all I ever did was loaf and watch TV."

"So ... ?"

"So, I decided not to let guilt rule me anymore."

"Wow! Glumbunny, I'm really proud of you."

"How about it, may I join you?"

"Absolutely!"

"Oh, one more thing."

"What's that, Glumbunny?"

"Bye, everyone, I've had a great time traveling through this book with you on the road to happiness."

Finally, I invite readers to contact me by email, pollyannan@aol.com. I promise to read all your comments and answer any questions.

I wish you success on your journey to happiness.

> *"We have what we seek. It is there*
> *all the time, and if we give it time, it will*
> *make itself known to us."*
>
> — Thomas Merton

RECOMMENDED READING

Bancom, John Q., *Baby Steps to Happiness*. Lancaster, PA: Starburst Publishers, 1996.

Bedard, Dr. Bob, *How To Be a Happier Person — Now*. Dexter, MI: Happiness Communications, 1988.

Benson, Herbert, MD, *Timeless Healing*. New York, NY: Fireside, 1996.

Bloomfield, Harold H., and Kory, Robert B., *Inner Joy*. New York, NY: Jove Publications, 1980.

Brandon, Nathaniel, *Six Pillars of Self Esteem*. New York, NY: Bantam Books, 1994.

Braun, Stephen, *The Science of Happiness*. New York, NY: John Wiley and Sons, Inc., 2000.

Carlson, Richard, *You Can Be Happy No Matter What*. San Rafael, CA: New World Library, 1992.

————, *You Can Feel Good Again*. New York, NY: Plume Printing, 1994.

————, *Don't Sweat the Small Stuff*. New York, NY: Hyperon, 1997.

————, *What About the Big Stuff?* New York, NY: Hyperon, 2002.

Cohn, Alan, *I Had It All the Time*. Haiku, HI: Alan Cohn Publications, 1995.

Cushnir Howard Raphael, *Unconditional Bliss*. Wheaton, IL: Quest Books, 2000.

Dalai Lama, H. H., and Cutler, Howard C., *The Art of Happiness*. New York, NY: Riverhead Books, 1998.

Dreaver, Jim, *The Way of Harmony*. New York, NY: Avon Books, Inc., 1999.

Dyer, Wayne W., *Your Erroneous Zones*. New York, NY: Funk and Wagnalls, 1976.

————, *Pulling Your Own Strings*. New York, NY: Thomas Y. Crowell Co., 1978.

————, *Real Magic*. New York, NY: HarperCollins Publishers, 1992.

————, *Wisdom of the Ages*. New York, NY: HarperCollins Publishers, 1998.

————, *There's a Spiritual Solution to Every Problem*. New York, NY: HarperCollins Publishers, 2001.

Ellis, Albert, and Becker, Irving, *A Guide to Personal Happiness*. North Hollywood, CA: Wilshire Book Co., 1982.

Finley, Guy, *The Secret of Letting Go*. St. Paul, MN: Llewellyn Press, 1990.

————, *Freedom From the Ties that Bind*. St. Paul, MN: Llewellyn Press, 1994.

Foster, Rick, and Hicks, Greg, *How We Choose To Be Happy*. New York, NY: G. P. Putnam's Sons Publishers, 1999.

Fulghum, Robert, *All I Really Need To Know I Learned In Kindergarten*. New York, NY: Villard Books, 1989.

Jampolsky, Gerald G., and Cirincione, Diane V., *Change Your Mind, Change Your Life*. New York, NY: Bantam Books, 1994.

Katie, Byron, *Loving What Is*. New York, NY: Harmony Books, 2002.

Kaufman, Barry Neil, *Happiness Is a Choice*. New York, NY: Ballantine Books, 1991.

Kehoe, John, *The Practice of Happiness*. Vancouver, B.C.: Zoetic, Inc., 1999.

Keyes Jr., Ken, *Discovering the Secrets of Happiness. Coos Bay, OR: Love Line Books, 1989.*

————, *Your Road Map to Lifelong Happiness*. Coos Bay, OR: Love Line Books, 1995.

Kingwell, Mark, *In Pursuit of Happiness*. New York, NY: Crown Publishers, 1998.

Levoy, Gregg, *Callings*. New York, NY: Three Rivers Press, 1997.

Lykken, David, *Happiness*. New York, NY: Golden Books, 1999.

McCready, Stuart (Ed.), *The Discovery of Happiness*. Naperville, IL: Sourcebooks, Inc., 2001.

McGinnis, Alan Loy, *The Power of Optimism*. San Francisco, CA: Harper and Row Publishers, 1990.

McGraw, Phillip C., *Self Matters*. New York, NY: Simon and Schuster Source, 2001.

Miller, Timothy, *How To Want What You Have*. New York, NY: Avon Books, 1995.

Myers, David G., *The Pursuit of Happiness*. New York, NY: William Morrow and Co., Inc., 1992.

Niven, David, *The 100 Simple Secrets of Happy People*. New York, NY: HarperCollins Publishers, Inc., 2000.

Null, Gary, *Choosing Joy*. New York, NY: Carroll and Graph Publishers, Inc., 1998.

O'Grady, Dennis, *Taking the Fear Out of Changing*. Holbrook, MA: Adams Media Corporation, 1994.

Page, Susan, *If We're So in Love, Why Aren't We Happy?* New York, NY: Harmony Press, 2002.

Pearsall, Paul, *Write Your Own Pleasure Prescription*. Alameda, CA:Hunter House, Inc., 1997.

————, *Super Joy*. New York, NY: Doubleday, 1998.

Porter, Eleanor H., *Pollyanna*. New York, NY: Dell Publishing, Inc., 1986.

Prager, Dennis, *Happiness Is a Serious Problem*. New York, NY: Regan Books, 1998.

Prather, Hugh, *How to Live in the World and Still Be Happy*. New York Beach, ME: Conari Press, 2002.

Ray, Veronica, *Choosing Happiness*. New York, NY: HarperCollins, 1991.

Resnick, Stella, *The Pleasure Zone*, Berkeley, CA: Conari Press, 1997.

Reynolds, Simon, *Become Happy in Eight Minutes*. New York, NY: Plume Books, 1996.

Rowland, Michael Domeyko, *Absolute Happiness*. Carson, CA: Hay House, 1993, 1995.

Russell, Bertrand, *The Conquest of Happiness*. New York, NY: Liveright Publishing Corporation, 1930.

Sahelian, Ray, *Be Happier Starting Now*. Marina Del Ray, CA: Be Happier Press, 1994.

Salmansohn, Karen, *How To Be Happy, Dammit*. Berkeley, CA: Celestial Arts, 2001.

Schwartz, Tony, *What Really Matters*. New York, NY: Bantam Books, 1996.

Seligman, Martin E. P., *Learned Optimism*. New York, NY: Alfred A. Knopf, 1991.

————, *Authentic Happiness*. New York, NY: The Free Press, 2002.

Sinetar, Marsha, *Living Happily Ever After*. New York, NY: Villard Books, 1990.

Tolle, Eckhart, *The Power of Now*. Novato, CA: New World Library, 1999.

Tsubota, Kazuo, *Gokigen — Choosing Happiness as a Strategy*. Tokyo, Japan, Sunmark Publishing, Inc., 2000.

Walsh, Roger, *Essential Spirituality*. New York, NY: John Wiley and Sons, Inc., 1999.

Wholey, Dennis, *Are You Happy?* Boston, MA: Houghton Miffin Co., 1986.

————, *The Miracle of Change*. New York, NY: Pocket Books, 1997.

APPENDIX

Happiness Keys: Self-Evaluation Scale

100													100
80													80
60													60
40													40
20													20
0													0

Awareness · Self-Like · Self-Esteem · Appreciation · Acceptance · Responsibility · Nonjudgement · Pollyanna's Game · Mistakes · Individuality · Perfection · Present Moment

IF YOU'D LIKE TO ORDER MORE COPIES OF:

HAPPY 4 LIFE

Here's How to Do It:

Call: 1-888-232-4444
or
Visit Trafford's website at: www.trafford.com

ISBN 1412000083-1

Edwards Brothers Malloy
Oxnard, CA USA
October 24, 2014